HARNESS YOUR INNER CEO

RISE INTO PASSION, PROSPERITY, AND EMPOWERMENT

Anxious Lotus Publications
Lake Worth, Fl 33467
Email: theanxiouslotus@gmail.com

ISBN: 978-1-7372503-1-9 (print)
ISBN: 978-1-7372503-2-6 (hardback)
ISBN: 978-1-7372503-0-2 (ebook)
ISBN: 978-1-7372503-3-3 (audiobook)

Ordering Information:
Special discounts are available on quantity purchases by corporations, associations, and others. For details, contact E: info@beccapowers.com, beccapowers.com, P: (561) 463-6400

HARNESS YOUR INNER CEO

RISE INTO PASSION, PROSPERITY, AND EMPOWERMENT

AWARD-WINNING FORTUNE 500 SALES EXECUTIVE

BECCA POWERS

FOREWORD BY NANCY LEVIN

DEDICATION

To my children and all the children who have suffered from the dysfunction, disempowerment, and sometimes dangerous slumber of adults. Waking up is the best thing I ever did. This book is dedicated to your resilience and unconditional love. I now understand that you thrive when I thrive.

TABLE OF CONTENTS

FOREWORD

BY NANCY LEVIN

Is there something you really, really want to do or have, but consistently talk yourself out of because it's "unrealistic?" Do you keep yourself so overscheduled and busy, even when you desperately need a break, because slowing down would mean you're lazy, irresponsible, and lack value? Are you fed up with watching other people lead fulfilling, meaningful, satisfying lives—making money doing what they love—while either wondering when it'll be your turn, or just believing it's not meant for you?

If any of these sound familiar, then it's time to ask yourself, "Isn't it time I harness my Inner CEO?!"

As an overachiever and people-pleaser who never wanted to rock the boat, I was constantly seeking external validation and approval. I put everyone else's wants, dreams, and needs before mine and prided myself in how much I could *do*, believing that would determine my worth. I spent my days managing the perceptions of others, projecting an image of perfection. In the process, I forgot something.

I forgot to live my own life. And that's no way to live.

1

This book you are holding is an invitation to your fully inhabited life, a map to the treasure of aliveness within you.

I've had the honor of witnessing Becca's profound evolution firsthand by coaching her privately as well as training her in my Levin Life Coach Academy certification program. In fact, her journey so powerfully and perfectly embodies what I call my Transformation Equation: Change = Vision + Choice + Action.

Becca is an embodied blend of business badass and self-help seeker with a palpable and contagious commitment to her own transformation. I've cherished the opportunity to hold her accountable to taking action in the direction of her desires.

Having coached thousands of people to embrace fear and welcome change through truth-telling, whether it be relationship transitions, switching careers, geographical relocations, or setting boundaries, to name a few, I've also made my own jumps that include a contentious divorce after a long-term marriage and quitting my prestigious position as Event Director at Hay House, Inc. to start my own business as a coach, author, and teacher. I can assure you that no matter what the external jump is, the internal jump is always a deepening of self-awareness, self-acceptance, self-compassion, self-forgiveness, self-love, and self-worth.

As I've written about in my books *Setting Boundaries Will Set You Free*, *Worthy, Permission to Put Yourself First*, and *Jump...And Your Life Will Appear*, it's time to stop packaging yourself to be digestible to others and live life on your own terms! It all begins with being willing to give yourself permission to consider yourself, and your own needs, *at least as much* as you consider everyone else. Then, considering your needs *more* than the needs of others. And then, consider your needs *first*!

When you open yourself up to having and receiving, you can celebrate your success instead of bonding with others over suffering. You can honor the space between no longer and not yet, even as you are still becoming.

My wish for you is that you'll let this book be a beacon, illuminating the path of what's possible (everything!). Becca courageously and transparently shares her personal traumas and triumphs and I invite you to find yourself in her impactful story as you embrace her methodology. This potent and practical gem of a book is a compass guiding you on the most sacred journey you'll ever take—truly owning your worth.

Nancy Levin
Boulder, Colorado
March 2021

INTRODUCTION

"I freaking quit. I can't believe I did it! Want to know what else I did?" I laughed to my best friend Monica. "I skip-leveled my boss and quit to *his* boss, the VP of sales. God, I have some balls!" I said through a snicker of amusement.

"Oh my God, Becca, what did he say?"

"Monica you'll never believe it," I replied. "Markeith told me that I am the CEO of my own life and I need to do what I feel is best. I'm telling you, Monica, my mind is blown!"

"That's incredible, Bec," Monica said. "How did he feel about the skip-level resignation?"

I knew why she asked: going over your boss's head is typically frowned upon in big corporate, and I knew this well. I was a regional sales manager for Dell, one of the largest tech companies in the world. Chain of command is a big thing in the tech world and I had just broken it.

"He handled it well, actually, and he understood why I'm leaving," I told her. Dell has a lot of smart, strategic, and seasoned leaders, and my VP of sales was one of those. Markeith understood that I had an offer from a company with the motto, "Putting People First," which aligned with my leadership philosophy. I had explained to Markeith that I would have the opportunity to sit on the company's weekly executive council and that I couldn't turn it down. It was an opportunity I would never get at Dell simply because the company was so big and I was too far down in middle management. When I resigned to Markeith, I knew he would get it. When he told me I was the CEO of my own life, I felt validated in my decision. He ended the conversation by telling me I'd always have a home at Dell.

"Now you've got to tell me how Calum handled it," said Monica.

I paused before answering. Calum was my regional sales director. I didn't trust him. I always felt he would do anything to make himself look good even at the expense of someone else. He never verbalized it, but it felt like he didn't respect the women leaders as much as he did the male leaders on our team, a theme I have run into more than once in my sales career. No matter how much a company like Dell promotes diversity, it always comes down to the individual to demonstrate it. With 20 years at Dell, he had too many good ole boy connections and was too centered on making himself look good for me to feel comfortable going to him first. I feared him marking me "not rehireable" because my quitting made him look bad. I knew it was safer to resign to Markeith.

I finally replied, "Calum was pissed, and he said the bottom line was that I should've resigned to him first. I told him I understood, and that I had to call Markeith for something else and then, whether wrong or right, I acted on instinct and decided to tell Markeith then and there."

I wrapped up the call with Monica and sat in my car for a moment. I allowed those words to flow through me, *"You are the CEO of your life."* They filled me with inspiration, motivation, and empowerment. I felt like I was walking on clouds as I went back to the building to notify my team that I was resigning.

I asked myself: What was possible for me if I was able to harness my inner CEO?

YOU ARE THE CEO OF YOUR LIFE

Before we get started, I want to ask you a few questions. Be super honest with your answers.

- Are you putting your job or your family's needs and desires ahead of what's important to you?

- Has your mind and body been sending you signals like anxiety, fatigue, and weight gain/loss?

- Are you in superhero mode: avoiding burnout by saying, "everything's fine" or "it is what it is" or "everything happens for a reason," while deep down knowing you are barely holding everything together?

- Are you stuck in a job or relationship that you know is unhealthy for you or that you know you've outgrown but can't seem to find the courage to leave?

- Are you feeling overworked, overstressed, overwhelmed, undervalued, unappreciated, or underestimated?

If you answered "yes" to any of the above, then you must keep reading. There is a reason this book ended up in your hands. Your life is asking you to reclaim it!

Being told that I am the CEO of my own life on that day back in 2013 would have a profound effect on me, but it didn't happen right away. I didn't fully understand that it meant I had to take charge. It wouldn't be until late 2016 that I finally started harnessing my inner CEO. My entire family and I now refer to the time in between as the "dark years," when I stepped out of my power to focus on everyone and everything except myself. We all suffered greatly.

By the time I was finally willing to admit that things were falling apart, my life was pretty well fucked. My marriage was on the fritz, my self-worth was embarrassingly low, my anxiety was so bad that I was diagnosed with two anxiety disorders, I had adult ADHD, and my hair was falling out in clumps. To top it all off, I was earning just over six figures yet was living paycheck to paycheck—with the occasional overdraft and all my credit cards maxed out. My life was a mess.

I had made my job the #1 priority and unwittingly became more absent to myself, my husband, and my kids than I care to admit. I was gone 12 hours a day and was not very emotionally present when I was home; consequently, my kids struggled with anxiety as well as felt my unintentional neglect. If those things weren't bad enough, I gained 35 pounds over the course of those three years and had lived so long under chronic stress that I ended up with an autoimmune disorder too. The cleanup my life required was monumental.

Although this felt like an insurmountable mountain of a task, I knew that if I could break it down into steps, it would be doable. And that's exactly what I did. After a few short months of recognizing and accepting that I was at rock bottom, my life began to take a drastic turn for the better. Committing to the process—no matter how long it took to complete the overhaul—was key. All in all, it took a little over two years to complete the transformation from surviving to thriving.

Throughout the course of this book, I will share all of my transformational secrets with you. From the dark years, I learned that when we step out of our power, stay rooted in low self-worth, and try to fulfill other people's visions of us—our life falls apart. Not only do we suffer but our loved ones suffer too. The craziest part about it is, *often we fall apart when we are trying so hard to hold it together.* The goal of this book is to give you practical steps that you can return to again and again to prioritize yourself and help you create a life you love and deserve.

My first power move after I reclaimed my self-worth from the toilet resulted in a $65,000 a year pay increase. I'm happy to report that after following the steps I'm about to share with you, my marriage is back on track and I've gone way beyond my goal of making $250,000 a year. My anxiety and ADHD are no longer running the show. I have healed myself holistically from the inside out and am off all medication. My husband and I built our dream home, are living debt free, and recently bought land for an as-yet-to-be-determined future vacation rental and dream home.

As I write this book, I am working for Cisco Systems amidst the COVID-19 global pandemic, social unrest for equality, and all the geopolitical issues that are in play in 2020. Cisco is another of the largest Tech companies in the world. Our CEO, Chuck Robbins, our chief sales and marketing officer, Gerri Elliott, and the rest of our leadership have demonstrated repeatedly that they put "People Before Profits." This is one of my internal mission statements that must be present and demonstrated for me to really enjoy and thrive in corporate America. I have been in complete awe with the way Cisco has risen to the occasion during these difficult times and I am proud to work for them.

COVID-19 and the isolation that has come with it have allowed me to come out of the writer's closet. Before starting this book I had spent over two decades writing with no one seeing or hearing a word I had written. I also reopened my life-coaching business: it was something I had closed when I stepped out of my power and was trying to please everyone else. After creating and following the steps that I outline in this book, I am more expansive than I have ever been and I am enjoying success and happiness—without chronic stress—way beyond my wildest dreams. There is so much to gain from harnessing your inner CEO. I can't wait for you to start your journey with me!

The steps I share in this book are the very same steps that I took to harness my inner CEO and get my life back on track. These are the same steps I now use with my clients: it's been incredible to see how their lives have started supporting them in the most meaningful and miraculous ways.

I will guide you through this step-by-step transformational process that I have used on myself and others. You will harness your inner CEO and reap all of the delightful rewards of igniting your power, passion, and prosperity. When you are in alignment with these elements, life blossoms for you in the most wonderful, unimaginable, and unpredictable ways. Today you are making the conscious choice to create a life that you love to live on your own terms. I'm so excited for you!

HOW THIS BOOK WORKS

Each chapter starts off with a story from my journey as a rock star sales executive making my way through life in the 21st century. I often use the context of my life story and the lessons I've learned through obstacles, ball-juggling, and chance encounters to illustrate how you might be able to apply the essence of these lessons to your own life.

In each chapter, following the personal story, you will find a section titled Putting It into Practice. This section distills the theme of the chapter into an actionable step. Each Putting It into Practice section includes an additional exercise and encourages you to think about how this chapter relates to your own life and the possibilities yet to be explored.

Finally, each chapter ends with a story of a particular person who has inspired me in a way that is supportive of the theme of the chapter. Each person has had an impact in my life whether it be client, colleague, friend, or family member. The lessons that each person has imprinted on me are echoed throughout the section, helping each chapter to close with an illustration of the step in action. Ultimately, the goal is to serve you, the reader, with another source of inspiration of how to apply the spirit of the chapter to help you create a life that thrives—from the inside out.

To get the most out of the concepts of these steps, other readers have found it helpful to read through this book in its entirety before completing the exercises, and then come back and focus on a chapter per week. This allows the essence of each chapter the space to create meaningful and lasting change. The inspiration for you to *Harness Your Inner CEO* is within the stories themselves. The art of Harnessing Your Inner CEO and rising into your power, passion, and prosperity is contained in the Putting It into Practice section which includes the exercises. There is an appendix in the back of this book that will reference the page number of the beginning of each Putting It into Practice section to make it easier to go back to.

You can also visit https://www.beccapowers.com/worksheetshyic as another option for quick access to the Putting It into Practice sections and exercises within the book.

PART ONE

POWER

As I look up at the sky
It dawns on me
That we are all born with it

This invisible force
That can unify
Or destroy

Duality in manifest

Do we influence
Or do we dominate

Do we own it
Or does someone else

Do we control it
Or are we controlled

This "It"
is called Power

Within us we have a force
So expansive and magnificent
When activated
We could
Change
The
World

"Power" by Becca Powers

01 / ASSESS THE HEALTH OF YOUR ENTERPRISE

"We cannot change what we are not aware of, and once we are aware, we cannot help but change."

—Sheryl Sandberg[1]

DELL IS ACQUIRING US

My heart dropped into my stomach as I stood in the cube of one of my coworkers, Erica, who also happened to be one of my best friends. The sales floor halted its daily roar of chatter, calls with customers, and random outbursts from coworkers. There was dead silence. I could feel the fear instantaneously. It was thick, it was palpable, and it was real. Then it was broken by a few gasps: just enough sound to break up the eeriness that only pure silence can produce on a sales floor.

---

1   Sheryl Sandberg, *Lean In: Women, Work, and the Will to Lead* (New York, NY: Knopf, 2013).

The rumors were true. Our CEO at Quest Software had just emailed the entire company that Dell, one of the largest tech companies in the world, had just acquired us. We would officially merge companies at the start of Dell's fiscal year, February 2013.

At the time that the acquisition was announced in October 2012, I was in a division of Quest Software called ScriptLogic Software located in Boca Raton, Florida. Our division had been acquired by Quest Software in 2008, but they had left our office of 150 people to run independently with very little interference. We knew that with Dell acquiring us, our little happy world within the walls of ScriptLogic Software would be coming to an end.

THE DAYS LEADING TO THE MERGER

Fear had taken over ScriptLogic Software. The leadership at Quest Software did roadshows to all their locations including ours. Their intention was to reduce the fear and panic that these announcements typically produce. Although the sentiment was nice, many of us who had experience with mergers and acquisitions knew that once the merger was complete, Quest Software as we knew it would have little control.

As the weeks turned into the months, the dynamic of our happy little work world was coming to a screeching halt and feathers were definitely ruffled. The sparrows that were skittish about receiving a severance package, or getting merged into a company the size of Dell, took it upon themselves to fly away and find new opportunities. The ostriches that feared looking for another job because the market in South Florida was too competitive, simply put their heads in the sand and continued on. The wise old owls who wanted a severance package stopped being top producers and reduced their efforts to mediocre at best, to increase their odds of getting a paid package to leave. Then there were the eagles—people like me and my friends and coworkers, Jessica and Will, who saw a ton of opportunity in the merger and were ready to spread our wings and fly with it. Dell can be one of those companies that's super hard to get into from the outside. Jessica, Will, and I had a twinkle in our eye at the idea of a more prosperous future with this new inside track.

With my eye on the prize of going into Dell for a continued career path, I raised my hand for leadership. I had been a sales leader multiple times before and I knew I could make a positive impact. My manager, who had also been a mentor of mine, was leaving to join a startup along with a half dozen other salespeople. With my manager leaving, I applied for the role as regional sales manager. I was offered the role and would transfer with that title into Dell.

> *Life Hack: Be willing to see opportunity when others can't.*

DELL DAY HAS ARRIVED

After six long months, it was Dell Day—the end of one era and the start of a new one. By the time Dell Day came around, our team was down to about 10 people from 25. Prior to the promotion I ranked among the top reps in the company alongside my friends Jessica and Will. Will was the top rep on a different sales team than the one Jessica and I were on. All of us were President's Club winners. Presidents' Clubs are, in essence, a winner's circle for the sales elite within a corporation. Depending on the corporation, to qualify you have to hit a minimum of 100 percent of your sales goals. In addition, you need to rank among the top one to five percent of the sellers within the organization to get the award of an all-expense-paid trip to a dream destination in a luxury hotel with a guest of your choice.

Having gotten the promotion to manager, I was excited to have Jessica—fellow President's Club winner—on my team; I knew that together we would crush it. I was lobbying for Will to come to my team as well. I wanted my team to have some instant success that would help ease the nerves of the remaining team members. That vision was short-lived. Will and Jessica's talents were recognized within the first couple weeks and Jessica was promoted into the position of outside sales executive. Will was about to receive a promotion to regional sales manager of his team. In tech, when you have a high skill set, you either go into executive level sales or you go into sales leadership.

With Will and Jessica promoted, my team was down to eight. Out of all the 2,500 Quest Software employees, my little team of eight people—along with another dozen supporting roles for our division—were immediately folded into the big machine of Dell. The rest of Quest Software stayed operating "as is" under the name Dell's Software Group. My team immediately received new leadership, a new culture, new products, and new systems—all while being expected to perform at the same level we used to.

Stress of the transition aside, I did love the Dell culture. Because of their size, they use a team selling model: for each team there is an overarching account manager and then sales specialists who correspond with a particular technology within Dell. It's a model I was familiar with, having formerly been a regional sales manager for Office Depot business accounts, which also had a specialist model. This selling model is a lot of fun if you enjoy working as part of a team, but it was a radical concept for a lot of the people on my team who were only used to being independent contributors.

Independent contributors are commonly hired into an organization as account managers, account executives, or sales executives. These are the most entrepreneurial roles within an organization and the titles are often interchangeable. Independent contributors are given a territory or segment of business that they are completely responsible for. This includes marketing, lead development, expanding wallet share within the customer's account, customer service, project management, partner management, forecasting, and anything else that is needed to get the job done. Because of the entrepreneurial nature of their job, independent contributors typically have half of their pay—if not more—attached to their sales performance.

Many on my team had never worked in a team selling environment before and did not adjust well to their new sales-specialist role. While sales specialists are still very entrepreneurial by nature, their focus is typically geared to a specific solution or service. They are like sales ninjas. They get called by the account manager to provide the detail needed for the customer to understand the depth of solutions and services offered by the company. As an account manager you are the one in charge and have ownership over the accounts. As a sales specialist you don't have primary account control. Giving up account control was a hard pill for my team to swallow, especially since none of them had chosen to be a sales specialist; it was forced on them via acquisition.

In addition to all those changes, the new management had more salespeople than allocated headcount for the new budget year. This meant that whoever didn't perform on my team either needed to be managed up or out. Those that didn't perform would be put on a performance improvement plan also known as a PIP.

While on the PIP you either successfully come off it by hitting the goals detailed in the plan— this would be considered being managed up—or, if you are unable to successfully hit the goals, you are managed out—better known as getting fired. With this news, my already stressed team received an extra layer of pressure that they just couldn't handle and things started to fall apart.

SAVING MYSELF MEANT LEAVING MY TEAM

I remember flying to Dell headquarters in Round Rock, Texas, for my first quarterly business review as a sales leader with Dell. I was nervous because my team's performance, back in Florida, had slipped since the merger. On the other hand, I was excited and proud of myself because I was already a regional sales manager for Dell at 34 years old. While in Round Rock, I met my new VP of sales, who laid out the strategy around folding our business into the big machine of Dell. I could see why this made the most sense and was starting to feel some relief. I felt more confident in supporting my team in the new conditions and I left Round Rock with renewed energy.

While at the Austin airport, I hit up the souvenir shop and bought a handful of "Keep Austin Weird" can koozies for my four kids and my husband, Jermey. Right before I checked out, I strolled over to the book section, feeling the desire to get lost in a story. One book on the shelf grabbed my attention—*It's Not About the Coffee* by Howard Behar, the former VP of Starbucks. I could feel myself being drawn to this book—I love Starbucks and I thought I could use some leadership guidance.

I devoured that book and reread it two or three times within the week. It basically says that Starbucks's success was never about its coffee—it was about its employees and their customers. When making a decision, the leadership at Starbucks constantly asked itself, "How does this impact our employees?"[2] If the decisions didn't serve the greater good of their employees and customers, the decision got axed. This philosophy awakened a personal mission mantra for me—People Before Profits. I had always felt this way as a leader, but I never broke it down into such a succinct phrase. People Before Profits would become one of my guiding principles.

As the months began to unfold, it became clear that this role at Dell wasn't an exact fit. With the approach taken in folding our division immediately into Dell, it left our team in Boca poised to fail. It wasn't intentional, Dell is a great company; it just didn't go down the way it was planned. My team's performance continued to decline. The stress of system change, culture change, product change, job style change, and pressure to perform all but paralyzed my team's performance.

I took time to explain to my upper management what was happening to our performance and why. Although they understood, we had goals to hit and my team wasn't hitting them. I was eventually forced to fire some of

---

2   Howard Behar, *It's Not About the Coffee: Lessons on Putting People First from a Life at Starbucks* (New York, NY: Portfolio, 2009).

the very people I had been hired with years earlier when we were Script-Logic Software.

My team felt they'd had an unfair hand dealt to them: they had to undergo immediate integration while the rest of Quest Software got to remain as is. The team had a right to feel that way, but unfortunately, the solutions that my team specialized in were in direct competition with Dell solutions. Dell wanted to unify the selling efforts by folding us into their team with the competitive solution.

As I began firing people from my team, my mission mantra—People Before Profits—was playing on repeat in my head. The more it played, the more I felt out of alignment. It was beginning to take its toll on my mental and emotional health because I felt like I was putting profits before my people.

I knew that it was time to assess the health of my personal enterprise—to see how things were running within the walls of "Becca Enterprises" and to determine if change was needed. After assessing the various departments of my life, I realized that if I stayed in my role with Dell it meant I would have to be out of alignment with myself, and I wasn't willing to do that.

You would think this would be an empowering moment, right? But it was far from that. I knew that in order to save myself, I had to leave my team. The thought of leaving my team defenseless and vulnerable drove me to tears. I also knew it was going to require my big brave. Big brave is a term I made up for needing to summon monumental courage to confront something I know is going to be emotional for me.

With the decision made to explore a new role either within or outside of Dell, it was time to start working on the internal process of embracing my big brave and to be willing to put my needs before my team's.

PUTTING IT INTO PRACTICE

Step One: Assess the Health of Your Enterprise

. . . .

In step one, we are going to observe and assess the overall health of your operations. In my story, I could feel that my job was no longer in an authentic alignment with myself. This riff between what I was experiencing and what I wanted to be experiencing was causing me a lot of stress. This stress was starting to bleed over into other areas of my life. I knew it was time for an evaluation of sorts.

Having an intimate understanding of where you are right now—not tomorrow or the next day or a month from now—is the first step in creating a life that supports you.

This can be really hard for many of us. It's hard to look at the dysfunction in our lives, whether it be our job, our marriage, our relationship with others, or the way we treat ourselves. The list goes on! It's much easier to consciously bypass, wish things to be better, or just flat out ignore the signs that life is off track.

Let's start to explore how your operations are running. I look at Becca Enterprises through the lens of four primary departments and I encourage you to look at [Your Name] Enterprises the same way.

Here are the four primary departments:

- Human Relationships

- Health and Wellness

- Profession and Purpose

- Prosperity and Abundance

INTRODUCTION TO YOUR HUMAN RELATIONSHIPS DEPARTMENT

We will be looking at the health of your enterprise through the lens of the human relationships department (HR). Your HR department has five subdepartments. Breaking it down into five subdepartments will give us insight into the areas that are most in need of optimization and support. Equally, we will be able to lean into the areas that are running well for strength and stability as we look to make some transitions and tweaks.

The five subdepartments in your human relationships department are:

- Relationship with Romantic Partner

- Relationships with Family and Friends

- Relationship with Work

- Relationship with Yourself

- Relationship with the Universe

Now that we have some understanding of the HR departments in your enterprise, let's see how things are running by taking an assessment.

EXERCISE: PRE-ASSESSMENT CHECK-IN

After reading the subdepartments:

- Which subdepartment do you feel is running the best?

- Which subdepartment do you feel needs the most attention?

This will provide a reference point after we complete the assessment to see how in tune you are with yourself.

HUMAN RELATIONSHIP (HR) DEPARTMENT

For each statement select the answer that feels the truest for you.

Relationship with Romantic Partner

1. I can express myself freely without fear of being criticized:

    (5) Always (4) Often (3) Sometimes (2) Seldom (1) Never

2. I am comfortable carving out alone time in my schedule:

    (5) Always (4) Often (3) Sometimes (2) Seldom (1) Never

3. I am physically and emotionally safe:

    (5) Always (4) Often (3) Sometimes (2) Seldom (1) Never

4. I feel supported, respected, and appreciated:

    (5) Always (4) Often (3) Sometimes (2) Seldom (1) Never

5. I feel loved and feel I am a priority:

    (5) Always (4) Often (3) Sometimes (2) Seldom (1) Never

Total Points: _____

Relationships with Family and Friends

1. I can express myself freely without fear of being criticized:

    (5) Always (4) Often (3) Sometimes (2) Seldom (1) Never

2. I am at ease when I'm around my family:

    (5) Always (4) Often (3) Sometimes (2) Seldom (1) Never

3. I am emotionally safe:

    (5) Always (4) Often (3) Sometimes (2) Seldom (1) Never

4. I feel like I matter and am loved:

    (5) Always (4) Often (3) Sometimes (2) Seldom (1) Never

5. I feel included and I feel I am a priority:

> (5) Always (4) Often (3) Sometimes (2) Seldom (1) Never

Total Points: _____

Relationship with Work

1. I can share my ideas freely without fear of being criticized:

> (5) Always (4) Often (3) Sometimes (2) Seldom (1) Never

2. I easily decline additional workloads and stay clear of overcommitting:

> (5) Always (4) Often (3) Sometimes (2) Seldom (1) Never

3. It's safe for me to connect with coworkers and build friendships:

> (5) Always (4) Often (3) Sometimes (2) Seldom (1) Never

4. I feel comfortable asking others for help when I'm stuck or have taken on too much:

> (5) Always (4) Often (3) Sometimes (2) Seldom (1) Never

5. My strengths and are talents are supported and utilized:

> (5) Always (4) Often (3) Sometimes (2) Seldom (1) Never

Total Points: _____

Relationship with Self

1. I find it easy to put my needs first:

> (5) Always (4) Often (3) Sometimes (2) Seldom (1) Never

2. I feel confident in my own skin:

> (5) Always (4) Often (3) Sometimes (2) Seldom (1) Never

3. I am comfortable being alone in my own presence:

> (5) Always (4) Often (3) Sometimes (2) Seldom (1) Never

4. I can look at myself and feel love and compassion:

    (5) Always (4) Often (3) Sometimes (2) Seldom (1) Never

5. I am willing to admit when I need help:

    (5) Always (4) Often (3) Sometimes (2) Seldom (1) Never

Total Points: _____

Relationship with the Universe

1. I feel connected to a presence greater than me:

    (5) Always (4) Often (3) Sometimes (2) Seldom   (1) Never

2. I trust my intuition and honor my red flags:

    (5) Always (4) Often (3) Sometimes (2) Seldom (1) Never

3. It's easy for me to recognize the signs my body gives me (both good and bad):

    (5) Always (4) Often (3) Sometimes (2) Seldom (1) Never

4. I have a relationship with my angels and spirit guides:

    (5) Always (4) Often (3) Sometimes (2) Seldom (1) Never

5. I believe the Universe supports me and is always reorganizing in the direction of my highest and greatest good:

    (5) Always (4) Often (3) Sometimes (2) Seldom (1) Never

Total Points: _____

Next, add the total from all subdepartments.

Total Department Points: _____

ASSESSMENT OUTCOME

Your HR Department Is Thriving:
Total Points between 96-125

Congratulations, you are harnessing your inner CEO! You are confident and able to prioritize yourself and your own needs. Focus your energy on the subdepartments that need a little bit of love and attention. This will help you continue to run your operations smoothly and keep you in front of setbacks. Follow the steps in this book to make any necessary changes to keep your culture thriving.

Your HR Department Could Use a Morale Boost:
Total Points between 66-95

You may be feeling a little overwhelmed and in need of some guidance. While some subdepartments may be running well, others subdepartments need a morale boost, but it won't be too difficult to get back on track.

Suggestion: One question you can ask yourself before making a decision is, "Does this decision support my energy, my time, and my health?"

Slowly, over time, the more frequently you can put your needs first, the more you will stop feeling out of alignment and stretched. The steps throughout this book will help reclaim your life. Your HR Department will be back to thriving in no time.

Your HR Department Is Struggling:
Total Points between 25-65

More than likely you are feeling anxiety, stress, and/or exhaustion regularly. Things feel like they are falling apart, and they may very well be. The vulnerability required to ask for help has been paralyzing.

You have been feeling stuck and unclear on how to get out of this state. You can give yourself a pat on the back for making the first step in taking care of yourself. This is a huge step and deserves recognition!

This book is meant to hold a space for you to feel supported and guided. As you transform out of fear, fatigue, and frustration into your power, passion, and prosperity, you will make positive changes one step at a time—ultimately harnessing your inner CEO. Commit to the process and you will see your HR department thrive, I promise!

After completing this section…

The subdepartment that is running the best is:

_____

The subdepartment that needs the most attention is:

_____

What surprised most about this exercise is:

_____

_____

You can return to the self-assessment anytime at:

www.beccapowers.com/worksheetshyic

GRANDMA WEST

My Grandma West is everything that girls are made of: sugar and spice and everything bold and beautiful. Raised on a farm in Indiana, she is the epitome of a bad ass: an equal mix of grit and guts. She had as many siblings as one hand can count and they grew up with no electricity. During her childhood, I've been told, her chores consisted of shoveling animal crap.

My grandma has fiery red hair and the personality to match. I remember being about four years old, standing outside my parent's house and waiting for my grandma to arrive. I loved her so much and I always got so excited when she came over. I knew when she was close: I could hear her. More accurately, I could hear her car. I knew that any second she would be pulling up in the Zoom-Zoom and she would take me on a quick trip around the block.

"Here she comes!" I exclaimed, jumping up and down. In her bright yellow 1978 Corvette with the windows down she came zipping down the street. My heart was racing. I was smiling ear to ear. I could barely contain myself. She pulled into the driveway and said, "Becca Ann, get in!" With a skip and a jump I wasted no time. I was in the Zoom-Zoom and ready to ride!

As I got older, I got to talk to Grandma about life. I always thought she was rich. She assured me she was but not in the way that I thought. Grandma told me that true richness lies within your relationships. That's why she always encouraged everyone in our family to work through their shit and remember that family comes first. Regardless of whatever dysfunction might run in the family, we are all super close. Multiple generations show up at our West family get-togethers—we come out in masses.

Grandma also said that happiness is more than just money. Happiness is about being able to wake up and enjoy the sun on your face. It's being able to take a walk and breathe in the sweet air and notice that you're doing it. It's being able to garden and realize that you and the plants share a common bond. (Side note, I did not get Grandma's green thumb; unfortunately, I kill plants.)

She and my grandfather worked hard for everything they had. While she was an avid dreamer—and boy could she dream—she taught me that you need to do so with both feet on the ground. She would often say something to me along the lines of "Becca Ann, you can shit in one hand and wish in the other and see which one fills up faster."

This confused me and made me laugh as a kid. As an adult, I totally get it. Although I do consider myself a master manifester, because of grandma

I also understand that dreaming needs to be accompanied with action. Wishing without action, in my experience, is just hope without a plan.

Grandma also taught me that if you don't take care of yourself, you can't take care of other people. She taught me that it was much more painful to allow things to go undiscussed, to tolerate the intolerable, and to not honor yourself and your relationships.

Somewhere along the way, I threw that nugget of wisdom out the window. I spent a good portion of my life putting everyone else's needs before my own. This caused complete chaos in multiple areas of my life. It's super important that we understand the health of our relationship with ourselves, the Universe, and others. This helps us make adjustments so that we align life to support us rather than deplete us. When life supports us, it allows us to self-actualize and realize our potential for health, wealth, and happiness.

When I was in high school, my grandma asked if I knew what I wanted to be when I graduated. I told her I really didn't have a clue, but I knew I wanted to make $100,000 a year. I remember her kind of smirking and said, "Becca Ann, I have all the faith in the world that you can. You're gonna need a better plan than 'no clue,' though."

I hit my first six figures when I was 30 years old. I was so proud, and I couldn't wait to call my grandma! I knew this conversation would be bittersweet: Grandma has dementia. She doesn't really remember our previous conversations anymore. Ten minutes after our conversation she won't remember that we had it. But Grandma does remember me and she remembers how much she loves me. She remembers all her grandkids for that matter. That is enough to fill my grandma love tank—it has to be.

Grandma's matriarchal wisdom has shaped me into the person I am. It's helped me be a dreamer. It's helped me prepare and work toward a desire—even when I didn't know how it was going to come to fruition. It's helped me be courageous in facing adversity instead of turning away from it.

Above all, Grandma made sure I understood the power in pausing when life goes sideways. She instilled the value of assessing myself, my ambitions, and the situations I was in, to see if I was in alignment with my truth. Grandma was referred to by her friends as Wild Wilma because of her fierceness and fire—she always called things as she saw them and wasn't afraid to voice her thoughts. Extremely independent to this day—she is 92 and living on her own—she taught me the importance of self-preservation. She would say things like, "Becca Ann, you need to take care of yourself; if you don't, no one else will."

I remembered Grandma's teachings as I faced the decision to leave my position at Dell. Grandma's grit empowered me to stand strong in my convictions, it gave permission to reassess and change direction, and it showed me how to make a plan and work toward it. Her guts empowered me to move boldly through life, it gave me permission to go for what I dreamed, and showed me that if I took care of and prioritized myself in the world as well as my relationships, life would support me in ways I hadn't yet imagined.

02 / ADMIT WHEN THINGS ARE FUCKED

"Stepping onto a brand-new path is difficult, but not more difficult than remaining in a situation, which is not nurturing to the whole woman."

—Maya Angelou

SOMETHING WAS DIFFERENT

It took me a while to figure out why my first response to a difficult situation used to be to power through it. Maybe it was because I grew up playing soccer. In sports you give 100 percent right to the end and you get patted on the back for it. Perhaps it was because I've been in sales since I was 18 and I've learned that resilience has a pretty nice fiscal reward. Or maybe it was because I'm a full-blown people pleaser and I love going over and beyond to get the accolades. Whatever the reason, it seemed like my default coping method (DCM) had been to power through tough situations.

33

When I began to respond differently this time around, I surprised myself. Something was different about this situation. I was pausing. I was reflecting. I was evaluating myself and my environment. I was leaning into my spiritual practice and going within for answers. I was able to admit to myself that although I was in love with the idea of working for Dell as a regional sales manager, something just wasn't fitting.

During my moments of reflection, I was so proud of the woman I had become. I was confident, committed, and clear. I was confident in my ability to make difficult decisions with grace. I was committed to my two mission mantras: 1. People Before Profits and 2. Make a Positive Impact on People and the Planet. I was clear on what was good for me and unwilling to sacrifice my health and mental wellness.

I ADMITTED IT

After much consideration, I admitted that things were fucked. Although this statement can be bold and jarring on the surface— it's for a reason. Our nervous systems need pattern interruption to help us create healthy change. It's been proven that the surprising nature of an unexpected curse word here and there can shock the system and get you to pop out of powering through things—or whatever other coping method you may use.

This is why the acclaimed motivational speaker and success strategist, Tony Robbins, strategically uses curse words. If you've ever seen him live, you know that he uses them often—but really only once or twice with the same person. Once he's got them shocked and has their attention, they're no longer in their default coping pattern and he is able to help them see new possibilities. Simply put, when used intentionally, curse words are pattern interrupters.

In building an enterprise that thrives, it's a crucial second step to admit when things aren't working. Can you imagine an enterprise spending all its efforts on employee surveys and getting feedback from consultants, and then refusing to admit when things are not working?

The best companies have crucial conversations early on in their change process. They do exactly what we're doing here. They assess what's working and not working and then they're willing to admit—no matter how painful it might be—that the things that are not working need to change. Without this change, their enterprise won't thrive. And if their enterprise doesn't thrive, they'll be down revenue. Admitting that change is needed is a game changer.

Standing at this crossroads with Dell, knowing the kind of outcomes I'd experienced with my "Power Through and It Will Work Out" (PTAI-WWO) responses, I was relieved that Grandma's wisdom about assessing situations was now taking the lead and I was willing to admit that things were fucked.

For me, I need a phrase as strong as "Admit When Things Are Fucked." You will see in this next flashback how, in my first marriage, I used the PTAIWWO. You will see how I bypassed the red flags, prevented myself from having crucial conversations, and enabled the cycle of dysfunction to continue.

> *Life Hack: Admitting change is needed is a game changer.*

TROUBLE WRITTEN ALL OVER IT

"Oh shit, are those cop lights?" I said to myself as my heart dropped in my chest. I was just leaving reggae night at one of my favorite local hangouts, the Old Key Lime House. "Talk about a buzzkill," I said under my breath.

I had needed this night out badly. I was grieving the state of my marriage to my high school sweetheart. Jack and I had met when I was 14 and he was 17. He was everything my dad hated—a high school dropout artist and musician with tattoos and a bad attitude. Looking back, the marriage had "trouble" written all over it, but with my rebellious nature, that's the guy I had to have. We partied our asses off throughout my high school and college years.

Somehow, my inner sense of responsibility and inner overachiever still did very well in the things that were important to me—like school, soccer, and work. After I graduated high school, I attended college part-time and worked full-time. When I was 18, Jack and I bought a condo and started living together. We had a blast partying; the drugs went from beer and pot to liquor and cocaine. It was all fun until it wasn't.

I was 20 when I had such a horrible come-down from the drugs that I tried to kill myself. The attempt was feeble—I took 25 Advil and drank a liter of Mountain Dew—but because I was high, that seemed like a winning combo. Thankfully, I wasn't thinking clearly enough to execute. Outside of my altered state, I really didn't want to die. But I remember bargaining with God that if he let me live through it, I would never do hard drugs again. I lived and I kept my end of the bargain because I knew I would never forget that feeling of wanting everything to be over, and not wanting to feel the pain of the human experience ever again.

Shortly after my embarrassing attempt at suicide, Jack got off the hard drugs too. With our acts cleaned up, we were both doing pretty well. He proposed to me, and I said, "Yes." I was 21 the July that we got married and by the following February we found out I was pregnant with our daughter, Tyler. We were in shock and also super excited. Tyler was born in August 2001. She brought so much joy to us. Not too long after that, I was pregnant with our son, Braydon. We were so happy.

With the addition of another child, we needed to evaluate where we should raise our kids. We decided to move away from Coral Spring, Florida, to a town in a nice suburban area in West Palm Beach. By the time we were ready to move out of our condo it had doubled in equity, so we could afford to buy a house. We bought a beautiful starter home with three bedrooms and two baths. It was perfect. Pregnant and all, with a toddler in tow, we excitedly made the move. My son was born in November 2003.

Not too long after the move, Jack wanted to define his career. As a brilliant artist, he decided to go into tattooing. I thought this was an excellent fit for him. Jack did well when he was able to lean into his craft, whether it was his talent for drawing or for music. He was never the nine-to-five type and I was happy to see him pursue something he enjoyed.

THE POWER THROUGH AND IT WILL WORK OUT METHOD

In hindsight, this was the beginning of the end. Once Jack began to tattoo for a living, he got sucked back into the culture of sex, drugs, and rock 'n' roll. His behavior started to become suspicious and erratic. He was no longer dependable. He would do things like forget to pick up the kids from daycare, or not come home for a couple nights in a row—and then come home and pretend everything was okay. If I called him out on his behavior and asked if he was doing drugs again, the finger always got pointed back at me as if I was overreacting or trying to control him. It was always my fault.

If you have ever lived with an addict, you have experienced this level of master manipulation. It is hard to tell what is real and what is an illusion when you are deep in it. Not knowing what to do in my situation with Jack was when I really leaned into PTAIWWO. I was terrified to make a significant change; the fear of being alone had such a hard-core grip on me that I would tremble at the very thought.

By the time I got pulled over by the cops, I had no energy to fight. I felt empty, broken, and lost. This was my first night out in months and I felt I deserved it. Jack had just gotten home after being gone for about three days and spending $1,000 we didn't have. I knew it would result in having to write another letter to his dad for financial assistance. The mere thought of needing to do that again made me feel extremely embarrassed and worthless.

My kids were home asleep when I had decided to go out. I needed to blow off a little steam. I texted my best friends, Monica and Sherri, and asked if they would meet me at Key Lime House for reggae night. They knew by the sheer act of my reaching out that they had to say yes. I sent a text to a few other good friends and they joined us as well.

I had a couple drinks spaced out over the evening—nothing crazy. Okay…I did have one shot but that was it. I knew my kids were at home and I needed to be responsible. I had a glass of water for every alcoholic drink. The night wasn't about drinking, it was about being connected to good friends and getting a chance to have fun. I love reggae music and Key Lime House has one of the best local reggae nights. I got to dance with my besties and hang with my friends. It was exactly what I needed to get a little wind back in my sails. The music stopped at midnight and it was time to go home.

As I was driving away from Key Lime House, I was feeling good for the first time in months. I wanted to put on Sublime to enjoy some upbeat tunes on the way home. As I reached over to the passenger side to grab the CD case, I took the steering wheel with me and slightly swerved my car to the right before I straightened back out with the CD case in hand.

ISN'T IT IRONIC

Now, with police lights in my rearview mirror I pulled over. The high I was enjoying—feeling like myself for the first time in ages—was now met with an equally intense low. What happened next was like an out-of-body experience.

The officer asked for my driver's license and insurance. I got the documents together and handed them to him. He asked, "Ma'am have you been drinking?" I replied with a very broken and defeated, "Yes." He asked, "How many do you think you've had?" I couldn't control the answer—"A few." As the words left my lips I wanted to start crying; the look on his face told me that things were not okay.

He asked me to step out of the car and perform a roadside sobriety test. I passed! I was so happy that this nightmare was about to be over and I could go back to listening to Sublime and get my butt home. Not so fast. Because I admitted to having "a few" on video, he had enough to arrest me and he did.

I was so emotionally broken and exhausted from my marriage that I had very little fight in me. I willingly complied with all his requests. I agreed to doing a breathalyzer and blew a .09. That's .01 over the legal limit and this cop was hell-bent to proceed with the arrest—telling me I had a half a beer too many. As he drove me downtown for my DUI booking, I began to share my story. By the time we got to jail, he was feeling really bad for arresting me but said unfortunately it was too late.

I sat down on the cold cell bench next to drug addicts, prostitutes, and thieves. I was overwhelmed with emotions and curled myself into a ball and began to sob. The worst part of all was that I had to call Jack to pick me up in the morning when I got released. I knew Jack would have little sympathy because the tables had ironically turned. I would often say to him, "One day I'm going to be picking you up from jail." Without missing a beat when he answered my call, he quoted Alanis Morrissette and said to me, "Isn't it ironic, don'tcha think?"[3]

That night in August 2005 served to be one of the pivotal moments beginning my shift into prioritizing myself and my kids. It forced me to come clean. I had to admit to Jack's dad that I had gotten a DUI. I also shared everything leading up to the DUI inclusive of his son doing drugs again—the reason we kept asking for money.

---

3   Alanis Morissette, "Ironic," written by Alanis Morissette for Jagged Little Pill, 1996.

Lucky for all of us, Jack's dad is an amazing man. He's been a steady role model and father figure for me and he's a heck of a grandpa. It was embarrassing, heartbreaking, and a relief to finally share that things were fucked. It sure beat the PTAIWWO method, which clearly wasn't working. The DUI was an awakening for me of sorts. It wasn't too long after this event that I realized our marriage was over. It was important to me that we end on good terms. After all, he was the father of my children and at one time had been my best friend. I tried my best to end our marriage as peacefully and respectfully as possible. No matter how conscious you are about things, divorce is a bitch on everyone.

Breaking stubborn old patterns is hard—but it's also completely possible. My PTAIWWO method ran deep in my being—it was my default coping mechanism. Unfortunately, I wasn't able to see another way until I hit an emotional rock bottom. That being said, I'd like to give a little insight to where this PTAIWWO method originated—and for that we need to take another leap back in time to meet Mom and Dad Powers.

THE GUITAR GOD AND GODDESS OF THE KEYS

My mom and my dad were hippies, like legit hippies. They were both masterful musicians. My dad was a Guitar God and my mom was the Goddess of the Keys—keyboard and piano. Together they were a powerful duo who could sing and play anything from Pink Floyd to Fleetwood Mac to Journey to Heart.

My brother and I grew up with Marshall stacks as end tables and every house we lived in had a dedicated jam room. When I was born, my parents had a popular cover band called Park Avenue that played the bar circuit in the Bloomington and Indianapolis areas of Indiana. I was told that they even opened for John Mellencamp way back in '78, when he was Johnny Cougar.

We had an amazing childhood filled with regular live music jams and bonfires with acoustic sessions. Love, peace, and happiness filled the air when they were playing. It was truly incredible. On the other side of that coin, they enjoyed partying. As the oldest, I took on the role of caretaker. I made sure that any random couch crasher had a blanket and pillow. I made sure all the cigarette butts were out and that all the beer cans were put in the trash.

MAMA DUKES

My mom struggled with depression and used alcohol as her magic elixir. For us as kids, this meant that some days were good and some days were bad. On any given day we really didn't know how it would go. My mom did the best she could with the way she chose to cope with life—numbing it out. She was great with some things: laundry, keeping the house clean, cooking dinner every night, making sure we had everything we needed for school, and she most certainly was soccer mom of the year. She loved cheering for her kids. She also ended every night and every phone call with an *I love you.*

On her good days, she would sing and dance around the house. If I walked in the front door and music was blaring, I knew mom was in a good mood. My mom embodied Stevie Nicks–like energy and had a mystical way about her that I adored. If she was in a really good mood, she played the piano and sang—happiness filled the air. Like Grandma West, my mom also had a love for fast cars. As early as I can remember she always had Ford Mustangs; she taught me how to drive in one of those Mustangs and passed the generational lead foot down to me as well. We are a family that loves fast cars and freedom. If she was happy, you would hear her racing through the neighborhood just like Grandma West used to do.

On her bad days, my mom was always numb. She wasn't emotionally available for my brother and me the way we needed her to be. Her patience was generally thin. There was always a large amount of screaming and yelling and there wasn't a whole lot of opportunity to approach her for guidance or softer conversations. She was tough and wanted us to be tough too. She would often say things like, "Suck it up," "Stop your blubbering," and "Stop being such a sissy." If you needed kindness and compassion you went to Dad.

As a kid I was resilient as hell. Mom's lack of emotional empathy didn't really bother me. I always knew she loved me and that she was dealing with her own demons. This is where my PTAIWWO method originated. My brother, on the other hand, needed more nourishment than Mom could give. He would often turn to me. Now when I look back, I feel bad. I realize at times I was as insensitive as my mom. I brushed him off as being annoying. I love my brother fiercely; I just wasn't able to make up for the lack of nurturing from mom. Rather than needing nurturing, I needed freedom—freedom from my home and the people who lived there. I wanted to be as independent as possible, explore the world, and everything in it. The PTAIWWO method gave me the coping mechanism to do exactly that.

DADDIO

When I was a little girl, my dad was my hero. Even into adulthood I idolized him. He was larger than life. He embodied the image of a rock star. In my eyes, he was legendary. Rebellious in nature and wise beyond his years, he was highly educated, spoke four languages, and was extremely sophisticated when he had to be. The son of Major General, Patrick W. Powers, and one of the first women aeronautical graduates from Purdue, Doris H. Powers, he was raised with high expectations.

My dad despised the affluent lifestyle and dreamed of being a guitar legend. He rebelled against his parents and took the path of freedom and music. A wrench got thrown in his plans when he fell in love with my mom and had two kids. Although his rock star dreams came to a screeching halt, my dad never regretted having us—I could tell.

He was extremely loving and warm with us. He was compassionate, kind, and even-tempered. He was engaged when he was home and put in time with my brother and me, from camping expeditions and family road trips to lots of storytelling at bedtime. He told stories and played us songs as nursery rhymes as we got ready for bed. My favorite was "Mr. Tambourine Man" by Bob Dylan.

As we got older, my dad worked by day as a civil engineer and by night as the lead guitarist in a band. He made time for my brother and me on the weekends—woven in between gigs and band practice. Dad and I spent countless hours fishing in the Everglades of South Florida. It was by far my favorite activity with him and I was proud to be his fishing buddy.

Although my dad never hit the fame he sought for his talent, he and his bands received countless awards and trophies. They would perform at fairs, festivals, and bars across the state. This left my brother and me home with my mom a lot. It's probably one of the reasons she was so pissed all the time. Someone needed to stay home with the kids and that someone was her. Because of that she was no longer in the band.

Dad's unwavering love and his ability to follow his dreams left a huge impression on me. It gave me the support I need to spread my wings and fly. I also learned the PTAIWWO method from him—he was a master at it. Being my dad's shadow, I quickly adopted it as my own.

THE WHITE-WINGED DOVE

I remember working for Sprint PCS and standing in the break room when I got the call from my dad. He said, "Redly, you need to come home now." This was the nickname he gave me the moment I was born and he saw my fiery red hair. He had always used it as a term of endearment with me. The tone in his voice scared the crap out of me. I could tell he wasn't mad but he was firm. My heart was racing as I sat in silence waiting to hear his next words.

"Your mom accidentally overdosed and stopped breathing. I was able to give her CPR but it's not likely she will make it. You need to come home," he said in a monotone voice.

I was able to get home to my dad in about 30 minutes. We waited for my brother to arrive so we could all go to the hospital together. When we arrived, we understood quickly that the likelihood of my mom surviving this horrific encounter with prescription drugs was slim. On a ventilator, she was pronounced brain dead.

The three of us were asked to consider letting her die naturally and signing a do not resuscitate form because—in the end—it would cause her to suffer more. We agreed that was the best decision. Within 12 hours of signing the DNR, she had crossed over and earned her white wings. It was October 22, 2002. I was 23, my brother was 21, and now we were motherless here on the Earth plane.

My mom's passing had me double down on my PTAIWWO method even more. It had me grip harder to my marriage to Jack; I was terrified at the thought of losing another relationship. I had an extremely hard time admitting things were fucked. It was as if that option didn't even exist. I believe this is why it took my getting arrested in 2005 to make me finally admit that things were spiraling out of control.

PUTTING IT INTO PRACTICE

Step Two: The Admit When Things Are Fucked Method
. . . .

There are many different default coping methods (DCM). None of them are wrong or right, so please don't judge yourself negatively. On the contrary, you are so resilient and strong that you created a DCM to survive your childhood. That's pretty incredible and you should pat yourself on the back. You did it, you survived!

The problem with our DCMs is that when we become adults, these out-dated survival systems are still sitting in the background running the show. They never got the memo that you aren't eight years old anymore. They never got a program upgrade from the program administrator—you.

Think of it like an application on your phone. The application runs the same program until it receives an upgrade. But what happens when your favorite application is falling behind in upgrades? It feels slow compared to other, newer apps. It hasn't adapted to new technology and may lack the ability to integrate with other apps. It starts to lose its ease of use because it's falling behind the times.

Now let's think of you as an app that gets an upgrade. The app is given a new program. It now has the ability to do things it didn't do before and you're excited to use it. It's able to connect and integrate with other apps making your life easier. Because of its ease of use, the app actually brings you some joy and limits your frustration.

Now, what if *you* were that app and all you needed was an upgraded program? Would you be willing to give yourself that upgrade? Wouldn't it be nice to feel joy, ease, and excitement? That's exactly the intention of this step: to help you write a new program so you can get that upgraded quality of life.

How do you know if you are due for an upgrade? In the last chapter, you were able to do an assessment on the health of your human resources de-partment. Particularly if the results of your assessment were "Your HR De-partment Needs a Morale Boost" or "Your HR Department Is Struggling," you have an indicator that a new program such as "The Admit When Things Are Fucked Method" (AWTAF) would be a welcomed upgrade.

Let's dive into your old method a little bit more before we prepare for a new one. As we start to bring the concept of DCM's to light, it's a good time to reflect. I want you to consider how you move through life when there are problems and when situations are spinning out of your control.

Do you:

- **Power Through**: Are you aware there is a problem and hope it will work out on its own if you keep pressing forward?

- **Control**: Do you like to control things: your life, your outcomes, other people?

- **Numb**: Do you choose to numb out problems with alcohol, work, or food?

- **Run**: Do you run from your problems, your life, and people in it when things get tough?

If you were to choose just one *default coping method* which one would you choose and why?

_____

_____

_____

_____

_____

How did this *default coping method* help you survive your childhood?

_____

_____

_____

_____

_____

Fast forward to today, describe how your *default coping method* has held you back as an adult.

_____

_____

_____

_____

_____

Now that we have a little context for how you've handled things in the past and the impact of your DCM, we'll move to the present and establish where you are today with a current situation or problem. Then I will guide you through the step-by-step process of the AWTAF and this will serve as the new program for your system upgrade.

Describe a current situation that is not going as planned or that is problematic:

_____

_____

_____

_____

_____

With a better understanding of how you operate and having identified a current situation or problem, we'll move into the next part—admitting when things are fucked. This doesn't mean your life is screwed up to the point it can't be fixed. I mentioned earlier that curse words, used strategically, are a pattern interrupter. That's exactly what the AWTAF method is meant to do: interrupt your old patterns and create a new supportive way for you to handle problems as they arise. It's meant to help you pause, re-calibrate, reconsider, and invite in possibility.

The AWTAF method is designed to help you with everything from daily aggravations to chronic problems to things completely outside your control (which is most things). It's about giving you a program upgrade that supports you today—in your current conditions—not your childhood conditions. It's about learning how to replace your old DCMs with a new one that helps you thrive.

EXERCISE

The Four-Step Process to the Admitting When Things are Fucked Method

. . . .

While some of the steps in this book require preparation and action, this one is more about acknowledging that your problems exist and letting go of how you think they will get resolved. Sounds simple on the surface but if it were that simple you wouldn't be stuck in your DCMs.

Here are the four steps in the AWTAF method:

- Step 1: **Willingness to admit** there is a problem and that you don't have control over other people, places, and things.

- Step 2: **Believing in possibility**—that there is an outcome you have not considered that supports you better.

- Step 3: **Giving the Universe permission** to intercede and bring in new possibilities that align to an outcome that supports your highest and greatest good and the highest and greatest good of others.

- Step 4: **Following the breadcrumbs** the Universe sends you.

Let's go back to the problem or situation you identified above, then we will apply the four steps to it by finishing the sentence. You can go to https://www.beccapowers.com/worksheetshyic

to print this worksheet and do this exercise as many times as you want for as many problems as you want. This is a practice meant for you to return to again and again.

There is huge power in writing it down and releasing it to the Universe. Once you are done filling it out, simply read it to yourself, preferably out loud, to complete the exercise.

- Step 1: I am willing to admit that I have no control over...

  _____

- Step 2: I believe in the possibility that this situation (write the problem summary) _____ _____, can be resolved in ways I haven't yet considered.

- Step 3: I give the Universe permission to support the resolution of (write the problem summary), _____

  _____

  _____, in the highest and greatest good of myself and the highest and greatest good of others.

- Step 4: I will follow the breadcrumbs the Universe sends.

  Note: This could include witnessing clearer gut feelings, hunches, changed behavior in others (without your involvement), unexpected resolution of an issue, new ideas and insight, and support you were not expecting. These are only a few examples.

  Write down some breadcrumb moments below:

  _____

  _____

Write down anything that comes up in the form of breadcrumbs. Anything that is new or different from what you typically experience is worthy of writing down. Acknowledgment of the breadcrumbs is key for your default coping method to accept this new method as it's program upgrade. The old program is not going to relinquish control until it knows that the new method is not only safe but that it works.

BRODIGGITY

My mom's passing took a toll on both my brother and me. I turned to my old trusty PTAIWWO method. My brother was more like my mom and chose to numb everything out. He was a restaurant manager and would work 60-plus hours a week. We barely saw each other because he was so busy.

A couple years after my mom died, my brother's best friend from childhood died in a tragic motorcycle accident. He was my brother's ride or die and by some twist of bad luck he also died in October. His death combined with my mom's unexpected passing really broke my brother—he started drinking to numb, to cope.

My brother spent many years just barely holding it together. Around 2011, after his life completely fell apart and he hit rock bottom, he began the process of going in and out of AA. He had many attempts at recovery and by the time we entered 2014 he finally had a full year under his belt.

That October I received another devastating phone call. Once again, I was at work. I was in meetings and had left my phone at my desk. When I arrived back at my desk, I had a few missed calls from my dad. I was happy that he was calling me on repeat because I thought he was finally feeling better. My dad wasn't sick per se; he had peripheral neuropathy and was in extreme chronic pain. He had been given morphine for years to manage the pain, then suddenly, due to new state laws, it was no longer available for pain management. The state did not provide him with a proper step-down plan either. That being said, my dad had taken his last morphine pill on Thursday night. He knew he was going to go through withdrawal and was not looking forward to it.

I had spoken to my dad the Friday before and he was not feeling well. He had asked if I could give him the weekend to get through this and allow him to rest. He said he would call me Monday. I agreed and gave him the space. When I saw three missed calls from him, I thought the old man was finally feeling better.

Excitedly, I called back and my stepmom answered. She told me through a steady stream of tears that my dad had passed away earlier that morning. I called my brother and let him know the news. Unexpectedly losing our dad would send us both into a downward spiral. My brother began drinking again and it would launch the start of my "dark years."

Recovering from these devastating blows would take concentrated effort to break free from old patterns and trauma. As I thought of someone who embodies the AWTAF method to illustrate this chapter theme, I immediately thought of my brother. My brother and his wife are both in recovery. If you saw them today you would not believe they were the same people who almost killed themselves with the severity of their addictions. In experiencing severe loss, both of them had chosen to cope with the pain by numbing out everything.

In 2016 or so, my brother met his wife, Lacey. They were both bouncing in and out of recovery. I remember when my brother told me about her: without even meeting her I totally judged the situation—"What the heck are two addicts doing together? This is going to be a disaster." But by the grace of God, they became each other's rocks. They were committed to each other and committed to recovery. Today they are sober and raising the most wonderful baby boy, Liam.

When I told my brother I was writing this book and that he was my inspiration for this chapter, he said, "Sis, for today I am. But it's not about me. It's about admitting that things are out of my control and giving it to the Big Man to handle. Today I remembered to do that. Tomorrow I may forget to admit that I'm an alcoholic. The day I forget to turn it over to God—or the Universe as you like to call it—I'll be fucked again." He wrapped it up by saying, "For today, I can be your inspiration."

03 / ACTIVATE YOUR SELF-WORTH

"Love yourself first and everything else falls into line. You really need to love yourself to get anything done in this world."

—Lucille Ball

PEOPLE BEFORE PROFITS

People Before Profits became more than a mantra to me. It became part of me. It became a guiding principle. I had something that I could check my motives, decisions, and next moves against. I mentioned

earlier that it had helped me gain clarity, confidence, and conviction. It gave me the ability to tap into internal strength and it was wildly refreshing.

Not needing validation from outside myself was new for me. It was empowering and thrilling for a recovering people pleaser. I was at the helm of Becca Enterprises and enjoyed this vantage point. As I embarked into uncharted territory, I eagerly looked to see what was on the horizon.

I'd been a participant in a local women's group and professional networking groups for some years; that was something I began doing when I started taking my career more seriously. Feeling empowered, I was more compelled to be vocal in my networking meetings. I began to speak up about the need for organizations to put people before profits. It was during this time—at one of these meetings—that my childhood best friend, Alysia, now a doctor of physical therapy, approached me to apply to PLP Healthcare.

I didn't know much about PLP Healthcare at the time. In fact, I had never heard of them. I acknowledged the recommendation. Initially, I didn't give this too much thought. She offered me one of their business cards. Alysia suggested I call them if I ever considered leaving Dell. She felt that PLP Healthcare and my leadership philosophy would make a good match. I found that statement weird because I had just recently come to terms with the fact that I wasn't happy in my current role.

As I walked away, there on the business card was the company slogan "Putting People First." There was my bread crumb. I was willing to follow it .

It's in these moments when it's up to us to follow the breadcrumbs and say "yes." Enamored of the spell of enchantment that had been cast over me by the sexiness of the Universe, I smiled. When I got back to the office, I emailed the recruiter on that business card and I wrote, "I am curious about exploring an opportunity with PLP Healthcare. I was referred to you by Alysia. Attached is my résumé."

> *Life Hack: Always have your résumé ready.*

SECOND TIME'S THE CHARM

Shortly after sending over my résumé, I received a call from the recruiter: they wanted to begin the interview process. Through the interviews I learned more about the core values behind PLP Healthcare, including how they view and treat their employees. The position I originally interviewed for was not an exact fit. The recruiter suggested we stay in touch because she knew of another managerial role that would soon open in another division of the company. Not more than a month later I got a call to interview for that position in FTP Travel, which specialized in staffing medical facilities with healthcare professionals who worked on short-term contracts.

On the day of my interview with FTP Travel, as I got out of my car, I saw smoke billowing over from the side of the building. It smelled like a cookout. I was curious, so I walked to that side of the building to see what was going on. There was the president of FTP Travel, cooking hot dogs for the entire division simply because it was National Hot Dog Day. On top of that he was wearing a freaking hot dog suit. I laughed so hard and couldn't believe what I was seeing!

The interview process consisted of 11 separate interviews. Several of these were second interviews with the same people—but nonetheless, 11 unique interviews. The company is very thorough about who they let into their leadership circle, and the more time I spent with the leadership at FTP Travel, the more I wanted to work there.

After completing the interviews, I finally received an offer for the role as a recruitment sales manager. I knew from the interview process that they did not pay as well as Dell but I was still shocked when I saw the offer. It was for almost a third less than I was currently making. I remember thinking, do I really want to take a pay cut? But, on the other hand, what was the likelihood of me getting another offer from a company that has a slogan like Putting People First?

As a leader at FTP Travel I would also have the opportunity to sit on the executive council that met weekly. I would get to see the process of how an organization makes decisions on behalf of their employees as a collective executive leadership team. This I saw as an invaluable opportunity that I might not get again.

I felt conflicted. I could stay true to my newly discovered north star of People Before Profits and take a pay cut. Or I could stay with Dell and be paid well and stick to my traditional PTAIWWO method—and we know how well that works for me.

DECISIONS, DECISIONS, DECISIONS

With the offer in hand, I knew I had some decisions to make. I was ready to put myself before my profits. I had something I really believed in. I also knew that accepting this position was a ginormous step in the direction of creating a culture within Becca Enterprise that had more purpose to it. This was more than just accepting a job. This was about me standing up for something I believed in.

As confident as I was feeling, the reality was I had four kids to consider. By this time I had remarried, and my husband Jermey and I were raising a blended family with two kids each. This wasn't a decision I would be making alone. I knew he would support me in whatever direction I wanted to go, but I needed to discuss the decision with him. I was very concerned about the financial impact that following my mission mantra would have, but I was super excited about the opportunity because it was aligned with my beliefs and it had the additional incentive of my sitting on the executive council once a week. I really felt like this was a once in a lifetime opportunity that I needed to harness.

I am the main breadwinner of the family, so even though I had this strong desire, I needed to make sure my family was secure. At the time of this decision, my husband was paying a very large sum in child support and, because he is a firefighter, a large portion of his income went to retirement—thank goodness, because retirement savings have not been a strong suit of mine. All that being said, losing a third of my income when I was raising four children during their school years was quite a strike against the balance sheet.

The decision didn't come easy. We had to sleep on it for several nights. But as my husband started to see me leaning to the side of practicality, he grabbed me by the shoulders and said, "Take the job." He told me that everything would be okay. That was the reinforcement I needed. With my husband on board it was time to harness my big brave. I would accept the position with FTP Travel and give Dell my notice.

HELMET CHECK
Decision Breakdown

I'm pausing the story for a moment, it's time for a helmet check. This is a phrase one of my boss's used to say to us to make sure we were thinking clearly and making good decisions. Right now, I bet you're probably thinking, "You go girl!" You may even have a little excitement for me and the journey I'm about to embark on. It seemed pretty clear that was the path I was supposed to take, right?

I'm not saying it wasn't the path I was supposed to take because it led me to where I am today. This path has been my greatest teacher, but it certainly was a bitch. In reflection, there was a major flaw in my plan. Can you guess what it was?

I was willing to earn less than I was worth. My willingness to do that was a clear sign that my self-worth wasn't being properly prioritized. I also learned that you can't rank an ideal or a belief before yourself. No matter how honorable that ideal might be. I'm going to repeat that in a different way—if you have a highlighter, here's a place to use it! *If you prioritize an ideal, person, place, or thing before you prioritize yourself, you are inviting dysfunction, disempowerment, and disruption into your life.* I mean, how can you be the CEO of your enterprise if you are unwilling to prioritize yourself and be at the helm of your operations?

MY SELF-WORTH BEGAN TO CRUMBLE

I know I'm foreshadowing that things were about to go sideways, however, if you read the Before We Get Started section at the beginning of this book, you already know something's coming. What's a good story without a little bit of drama, right?

The intention of this book is to inspire you and give you the steps to be the CEO of your own life. If your self-worth is low and you are unable to prioritize yourself over other people and beliefs, your enterprise will never thrive. I realized that self-confidence and self-worth are not the same thing. While my confidence was high, underneath it all I didn't value myself. This has taught me that there is a direct correlation between our self-worth and our net worth. In addition, how we prioritize things is evident in our level of self-worth.

The mission mantra of People Before Profits felt so noble and honorable. I believed I could make a difference and make a positive impact for the people that work for corporate America. I was so blinded by my mission mantra that I sacrificed myself. In sacrificing myself I was unable to make the impact I wanted. Instead of being the powerful leader that I was—I stepped out of my authentic power and let an ideal lead rather than myself. A crumbling mistake.

THE LADDER OF SELF-WORTH

Structure is a beautiful thing for building an enterprise that thrives. It helps us understand what things would, should, or could look like. I'm not one that likes rigidness or constriction in any way. Because of that, I've always preferred structure over rules. I'm rebellious by nature and I like to break rules. Structure on the other hand is like a helpful suggestion in the direction we're going. Structure for me is like the foundation of a house.

We can't very well build an incredibly thriving culture and enterprise without self-worth as our foundation. To create this thriving culture we must activate our self-worth. For many, our self-worth gets shattered in childhood. If not in childhood, then by an ex-boyfriend or a horrible boss. Somewhere along the way our self-worth is impacted.

In the process of putting myself back together piece by piece, I was able to get intimate with my beliefs about self-worth—both the highs and the lows. I've learned that it is critical to understand the order in which you prioritize yourself in relation to the other aspects of your life. *You must be at the top.*

I've created the Ladder of Self-Worth to help give you structure around the order in which things should be prioritized for your culture to thrive.

The Ladder of Self- Worth:

1. You
2. The Universe
3. Intimate Relationships
4. Other People
5. Beliefs, Career, Money, Etc.

When these elements get out of order, our foundation gets cracks in it. It subjects our enterprise to the risk of going from thriving to surviving. I wish that back then someone had taught me about self-worth and the order in which things should be prioritized to maintain a healthy operation.

As you will see, as we continue into my epic career adventure, the moment I put the "or" between knowing what I am worth monetarily and my mission mantra—my self-worth took a negative hit. I have learned that "or" can often disempower us whereas "and" oftentimes empowers us. In this specific decision process, all I saw was the "or." The "and" was never an option. I felt I either had to choose my mission mantra "or" take a pay cut and lower my value. Which one would I choose—I chose my mission mantra. My foundation just got a crack.

PUTTING IT INTO PRACTICE
Step 3: Activate Your Self-Worth
....

If I had to choose again, I would choose my mission mantra AND honoring the amount of pay I was worth. I would not choose sacrificing one for the other. If FTP Travel was not able to pay the amount I was worth, then the job search must continue. Until I found a role that supported my mission mantra and was willing to pay me what I was worth, I wouldn't settle.

Here is another look at The Ladder of Self-Worth:

1. You

2. The Universe

3. Close Family and Friends

4. Other People

5. Beliefs, Career, Money Etc.

At the time I made this decision to work at FTP Travel, my Ladder of Self-Worth looked as follows:

1. Beliefs, Career, Money, Etc.

2. Intimate Relationships

3. The Universe

4. Other People

5. Me

Realizing my order of things was wrong was a hard pill to swallow. It still causes me discomfort to acknowledge that I had things so mixed up from a priority perspective. In hindsight, I really needed to apply The AWTAF method to my Ladder of Self-Worth. The only problem was I didn't know the rungs in my ladder were in the wrong order. To admit that things are fucked you need the awareness that they are.

In this section, we are going to explore the rungs of the Ladder of Self-Worth one rung at a time. As we move into the exercise, we will start to identify what your Ladder of Self-Worth currently looks like and how we might go about changing the order of your rungs. To harness your inner CEO, you need to activate your self-worth, and that's exactly what we are about to do.

THE LADDER OF SELF-WORTH—BREAKDOWN OF THE RUNGS:

Rung One—You: For your enterprise to thrive, you need to be at the top. Now this may seem selfish but I assure you it's not. When you put yourself as a priority, it gives you more energy and capacity to take care of everything else. This is similar to how we are told to put our oxygen mask on first, before we help others with theirs, in the event of an emergency on an airplane. Same concept here, you won't be any use to others if you're not able to help yourself first.

Rung Two—The Universe: Depending on your religious upbringing this might feel out of place. You might want to put the Universe or God first. This is how I felt when I first learned this concept. Then I started thinking about it as a mother to children. I would never want my children to put my needs before their own. If they did so they would never reach their full potential, they would always be holding themselves back. I would want them to put their needs first and allow me the opportunity to support them. I think of it like that. The Universe or God would never ask you to sacrifice your needs to prove your faith; rather, they ask that you lean on the Universe or God for support and give them permission to help you.

And if you aren't there yet in your beliefs about the Universe that's okay too. Experiment and try it. You might find that things work a little better.

Rung Three—Intimate Relationships: This one is super tricky for a lot of people. We often want to put lovers, parents, kids, and close loved ones above ourselves. It feels noble and oftentimes feels like it's what we are supposed to. Our lines between where we stop and where another begins are blurry. Self-sacrifice leads to suffering. This is why You and the Universe come before rung three: so that you can be fully present with this group of people. You will find that they thrive even more when you thrive.

Rung Four—Other People: If you are anything like me and seek validation and approval from others, like your boss, a coach, your peers, you may put the needs of others before your own. This is a slippery slope into self-sabotage and suffering. And there is no end in sight because people will keep popping into your life. You can stay stuck in this rung for a long time if you aren't mindful that you have a tendency to people please. Your willingness to help others until the point of chronic fatigue is a real side effect of putting others' needs before your own. This is why it's important to put yourself at the top of the priority ladder.

Rung Five—Beliefs, Career, Money, Etc.: While beliefs, your career, and making money are extremely important they shouldn't take the lead over human beings, most notably, you. There's an irony in my belief of People Before Profits. I believed this so hard until the point of self-sabotage. For example, my putting that belief before myself was actually my putting Belief Before People (that person was me). It was the opposite of the very thing I was advocating for People Before (Insert Subject). As a result, I ended up inviting dysfunction, disempowerment, and disruption into my life, proving that there is a reason that you need to put yourself before beliefs, career, money, and other things.

Now that you have an understanding of the rungs on the Ladder of Self-Worth, what stood out to you the most about what they mean and the order they are in?

_____

_____

_____

Looking back at your results from the assessment you did in chapter 1, what relationships are you prioritizing above yourself?

_____

_____

_____

Knowing what you know now of the order of the rungs, how could your life benefit by reorganizing the rungs on your Ladder of Self-Worth?

_____

_____

_____

EXERCISE

Reorganizing Your Ladder of Self-Worth

. . . .

Before we can reorganize, we need to understand where we are. In the exercise below, write down the current order of your rungs on the Ladder of Self-Worth.

Here are the rung titles for you to use to fill in the blanks below:

You—The Universe—Intimate Relationships—Other People—Beliefs, Career, Money, Etc.

From the options above, write the title of the rung next to the number that represents how you currently prioritize these options, with the number 1 representing the highest prioritization and the number 5 representing the lowest prioritization.

Your Current Ladder of Self-Worth:

1.

2.

3.

4.

5.

After completing your ladder, what realizations do you have about your current order of things?

_____

_____

_____

Do you have any reservations about putting yourself first? If so, what are they?

_____

_____

_____

In activating your self-worth and starting to consider yourself at least as much as you consider others, what aspects of your life do you feel will improve?

_____

_____

_____

You can return to the exercise anytime at: https://www.beccapowers.com/worksheetshyic

TYLER SKY

Tyler Sky. Every time I write it, say it, or read her first and middle name together I get butterflies, the same way I did when I first found out I was pregnant with her. She is 19 now and in college. Watching her grow up has been one of the most amazing accomplishments of my life. When I think about boundaries and putting yourself first, she is the first person that pops into my mind.

Ever since she was a baby, I've told her she was capable of anything. I told her she deserved to be treated well and if she wasn't, she needed to speak up. I taught her how to stand up when things are wrong and to stand up for what she believes in and to never be afraid to say "no," and to mean it! She never second guessed these things. They resonated as truth. As a result, she has become quite the activist.

Tyler also was naturally born with independence, individuality, and owning her worth. From the time she was an infant she would cry if you held her too long. She would much prefer to be held and cuddled during her awake time. Come sleep time she wanted her own space. As a toddler, she would want to play with her dad and then want to go play by herself and do her own thing. She never had a problem telling anyone "no." Mostly it came from a very genuine and authentic place and didn't come across as rude or inappropriate. I remember thinking: Is this normal for a child?

As she continued to grow into her grade school years, she was still very much able to say what she meant without twisting her words to appease an adult. She was never disrespectful but always clear that she knew where she stopped and they began.

Then we started to layer in a divorce, a stepfamily, and friends. Tyler was always seen as the courageous one of the kids. If something needed to be said on behalf of the kids, it was Tyler who said it. If someone was being treated unfairly, it was Tyler who lobbied for their justice. She always seemed fearless.

Into her preteens and teens, life began to throw its curveballs—some minor and some major. She faced some unfair punishments from us parents. Although she often complied with the punishments such as grounding, no phone, etc. it did not go without being voiced that the situation was unfair.

No matter the situation and the toughness that surrounded it, Tyler has stood up for herself to peers as well as adults. At 19 she is still clear on what's wrong and right and where she stops and where others begin.

I'm beyond grateful that between her being born with a natural tact for boundaries and me telling her—since birth—the worth of her standing up for herself, she puts herself at the top of the Self-Worth Ladder—self-worth fully activated.

A MESSAGE TO PARENTS:

Tell your children that they are worthy of love, respect, and of being treated well. They are listening. Provide them a safe place to tell you everything and anything. They need to feel heard. I have done many things wrong in my parenting, trust me. But the one thing I did do right was instill worthiness in my children. Tyler is proof that we can raise kids differently than we were raised. Through them and the work that we do on ourselves, we can break the cycles of dysfunction and do our part to create a better planet for the generations to come.

04 / OWNERSHIP CREATES OPPORTUNITY

"You either walk into your story and own your truth, or you live outside of your story, hustling for your worthiness."

—Brené Brown[4]

| TELLING MY DELL TEAM

With the decision made to leave Dell to go to FTP Travel, and the resignation formally given to Markeith and Calum, it was time to tell my team. I remember standing at the front of the room at Dell with seven people staring at me. Seven people that had been my coworkers, friends, and that now reported to me. They were real humans who were going to be affected

---

4   Brené Brown, "In You Must Go: Harnessing the Force by Owning Our Own Stories," Brené Brown, May 4, 2018, https://brenebrown.com/blog/2018/05/04/in-you-must-go-harnessing-the-force-by-owning-our-stories/.

by my resignation. Looking into their eyes, I felt like a horrible person for leaving them.

My heart was pounding. My palms were starting to sweat. My mind was racing, searching for the right words to say. Even though I was excited about my new role. I knew that leaving was going to leave them unprotected. I had already heard rumors indicating that if I wasn't there, executive leadership was probably going to lay off the Boca Raton team.

One of my good friends and peers had shared with me that there was a lot of concern as to whether the Boca team was going to be able to perform. Guilt popped in. I started questioning my decision again, right there in front of the room. I knew that I had made the right decision and I needed to stay focused. I embraced my big brave, shook it off, and took a deep breath. I knew I had to stand in my power and own my decision to leave.

My team knew something was wrong. I never held team meetings on Wednesdays. I could sense their fear and they could sense my awkwardness. To be honest, I think they thought I was going to let them know that we were all being laid off. I realized it when their first response upon hearing that I was leaving was relief. Once they processed that they were staying and I was going, the looks of sadness started. We had all been through so much together. I think half the team was really happy for me and knew that our conditions were bad and that I needed to go; the other half felt immediately vulnerable with the announcement of my departure. Both views are fair and valid. I assured them I would do everything I could during my last two weeks to set them up for success. During those two weeks I was asked to reconsider and stay. I declined. I was committed and owning my decision.

A WHOLE NEW WORLD

I was entering a whole new world and was loving the freshness of it. I knew this job in healthcare staffing would be different than the tech jobs

I had. In the tech industry, especially in sales, the office lifestyle is rather transient. Some days you're in the office, some days you're traveling, and some days you work from home. There is a level of freedom that comes with working in tech. Working as a sales manager for FTP Travel, I would be in the office daily. I had welcomed the change because it meant that I would not be traveling overnight anymore and, with my kids being middle-school age, the thought of being home every night made me feel like I was putting my kids as a priority.

All this freshness was met with an equal amount of nervousness. This whole new world was completely different than the one that I was used to. I had no inside connections, no proven history of being a badass within the walls of the job. I was starting everything from scratch. I had to learn the people, the processes, and the policies. And I can't forget the politics! Every enterprise has them.

The first couple months were lovely. The employees were warm-hearted, smiled a lot, and proudly wore their Putting People First shirts displaying the company slogan. I had spent my first few months training for the new role. One of the tasks I had been given was to spend some time in the role of the recruiter. Since I would be managing a team of recruiters, it made sense for me to have an intimate knowledge of their role and their sales process.

As my new hire onboarding came to an end, fear crept in. I began to question whether I had made the right decision. Although I was enjoying the new role and loved the messaging of the company, I was missing the strategic fast-paced environment of tech. As I started to waiver in my conviction, I remembered something one of my former VPs of sales had told me, "Ownership creates opportunity."

This thought empowered me to recommit to my decision. This statement had proven itself true on more than one occasion. Here's what I've learned from it—if you are wishy-washy, people see it. They feel it. They don't follow your lead. They don't trust you. Own your mistakes, own your successes, and own your decisions. The power of your convictions will provide others with clarity and confidence. Own it and they will follow your lead. Own it and they trust you. Own it and see new opportunities unfold.

I was grateful that I was anchoring back into this message. Over the years, I have created a three-step process for owning situations and decisions I have made.

Three Steps to Owning a Decision:

1. Stand behind the decision.

2. Identify some supportive folks to help navigate the impact of the decision.

3. If things go wrong, give yourself permission to choose again.

Life Hack: Ownership creates new opportunities.

STAND BEHIND MY DECISION

I had learned to be kinder to myself over the years. Earlier in my career and in my late 20s, I really beat myself up over my decisions. It was as if I was supposed to have some superpower of perfect decision-making. In reality, this rigid view was self-sabotaging. I would beat myself up as if I wasn't smart enough or aware enough and it would really lower my sense of self-worth. This pattern was one I was able to recognize and put a stop to. Decisions can go wrong, but I don't believe we go into them hoping they go horribly sideways. I believe we go into making a decision based upon the information we have at that time, and we hope it goes well.

As the doubt began to surface in my decision to leave the tech industry, I had to re-center myself. I made the decision to go to FTP Travel with the information I had at that time—with the beliefs that I had. In hindsight I would have made a different decision but I didn't have hindsight yet. I had the present moment and it required me to stand behind my decision. My self-esteem needed me to stand behind my decision. My sanity needed me to stand behind my decision. And my family needed me to stand behind my decision.

I began to review the top reasons I took the role with FTP Travel:

1. It aligned to my mission mantra: People Before Profits.
2. I got to be at the weekly executive council meeting.
3. I would be home every night.
4. I believed in the leadership team.

As I reviewed the reasons, my fear began to slip away. I felt confident in my reasons for changing industries and believed that I made the right decision. To this day when tech leaders ask me in an interview process, "Why did you leave tech and go to healthcare staffing?" I reply confidently with those four answers every time. They never question that response and most say, "I can certainly understand why you did that." Conversation over. My ownership of my decision supported me then and has continued to support me as new opportunities surfaced.

Feeling good about my decisions again, it was time to build some support to help me stay on track in case doubt creeped back in.

I CREATED MY FAN CLUB TO STAY CONFIDENT

Throughout my years in sales—as well as in personal life—creating a support network has been one of my natural go-tos, helping me keep my spirits up as I work through things. I knew I needed to stand behind this decision because ownership would create opportunity. I didn't know what exactly would be coming my way. I did know, however, that my conviction would awaken possibility. From there, I knew I would follow the breadcrumbs that the Universe provided me.

It was time to assemble my support group: my fan club as I like to call it. I wanted to select three people who knew business, who knew me and how I operate, and who supported my success and breaking glass ceilings. I have learned—having been backstabbed, hurt, and held back by letting the wrong people get too close—that the selection process in creating a fan club matters. Carrying past lessons learned forward with me into the moment, I began to select the three people I knew without a doubt would be my biggest fans.

The first person I picked was Monica—you remember her as my best friend from the introduction. She is one person who I allow myself to be extremely vulnerable with. I tell her everything no matter how ugly it is. She is always there with humor and love—*never* judgment. We have been able to laugh our way through some pretty dramatic life experiences. Our humor can be dark at times and it's pretty damn funny. Monica by profession is a clinical psychologist. She's also very spiritual and has training in past-life regression. I knew she would offer me good perspectives as well as support.

Next up was Jessica, my badass friend from Dell who got promoted within the first three weeks of the merger. Jessica is what I call a master manifester. We have been manifesting together for over a decade. I wish we had written down all the miracles we've witnessed because it would be incredible to share! Jessica is Catholic; her faith is unwavering and absolutely gorgeous. Her ability to see things clearly, her conviction in her beliefs, and her confidence make her a "hell, yes!" member of my fan club. Jessica is also protective: if she sees you're being harmed or mistreated she'll tell it like it is and tell you that you need to get the fuck away from it. Everyone needs a Jessica in their life.

Last but not least, is my beautiful friend Erica, who you met at the start of Chapter 1. Erica and I have such a wonderful harmony that we often say we brain-share because we feed off our shared energy so much. She's a wonderful mother and a brilliant creator: an amazing jewelry maker. The color and jewel combinations on her bracelets and necklaces are dazzling—I want to wear everything she makes all the time. We bond over this because I, too, enjoy creative expression in the form of creating yoga-inspired T-shirts. That's how my clothing brand, Yoga-Lush, was born. The enterprise is on its third name but I've been creating T-shirts since 2014. Erica was an absolute anchor in assuring me that I hadn't lost my creative side while I was chasing my career. She is a Christian and extremely faithful.

PRAYER CLUB BEFORE FAN CLUB

I want to share a little story of just how magical support can be when it comes from the right people. There's a reason I picked Jessica and Erica over some of my other friends and mentors. When Jessica, Erica, and I worked together at Dell, we bonded over our spiritual beliefs. Although we have different approaches, we all believe in the power of prayer. We would pray over our sales goals and ask the Universe to support us in achieving them.

For example, there was a time in 2011 when I was $40,000 away from hitting my annual sales goal. It was already December and there were only two weeks left in our fiscal year. I had worked so hard that not having hit my quota had me in tears. I remember heading toward the bathroom ready to cry one day when Jessica saw me. She said, "No girl, we aren't doing this today. Let's get Erica and go to lunch. We're bringing our Bibles and you bring your miracle book." So, we grabbed some lunch and went to a park.

Jessica always led us in prayer. She would often say, "When two or more people pray together, God is present." She began to pray. She asked God to remove any obstacles that might be in my way and to provide a new path so that I could see. She asked God to bless all of our families with prosperity as we closed out the year of 2011. With the three of us being as connected as we were in our faith, we knew the Universe was supporting us that day.

I know that chasing $40,000 to hit my sales goal may sound superficial, but if you're in sales, your entire identity and the following year's employment is based upon how you perform. Another thing that made this financial goal so emotional for me was that that year's President's Club trip was Kauai, Hawaii. I was $40,000 away from a free trip to Hawaii with Jermey. At that point in time, he was my fiancé. You better believe I was praying for a miracle—we needed that vacation!

Two weeks passed after Erica, Jessica, and I had our little prayer circle during lunch. I had closed every order I possibly could. I was now $20,000 away from my goal and it was the last sales day of the year. Around 2:00 o'clock that afternoon I started to clean my desk, wipe it down, disinfect it so that I could come into 2012 with a fresh start. But as I was wiping and rearranging things, I got an email about an order from an account that I didn't think would make it. The subject line said, "You're going to Hawaii!"

I remember sitting there with a look of disbelief on my face. Attached in the email was an order for $60,000. My contact at this account said, "I didn't want to get your hopes up, so I didn't reply until I knew we could do it."

If you have ever worked in corporate America I want you to envision sitting in your cube, staring at your computer, and having the best news *ever* come on the screen. Imagine the response you'd get when you'd say what I was about to say—out loud—"Are you fucking kidding me?!" as my excitement started to rise. My teammates in the cube had no idea whether it was a good call out or a bad call out. Everyone started asking, "Bec, are you okay?"

When I shook off the shock, I shouted as loud as I could, "I'm going to Hawaii!" I couldn't even control my next response. I threw my arms in a V for victory, stood up from my desk, and ran a victory lap around the sales floor, shouting repeatedly, "I'm going to Hawaii!!" I was so excited.

This is one of my more vivid memories of the power behind our little prayer club. With Jessica and Erica now in my fan club, I felt confident that I would be able to navigate my new role at FTP Travel with a lot more ease and clarity. Add in Monica and her unwavering support, I felt stronger than ever in my ability to stand tall in my decision.

PERMISSION TO CHOOSE AGAIN

Next on my list for fully owning this decision was to give myself permission to choose again. Sometimes we get the decision right and we can celebrate the success that it has brought us. Other times we get it wrong and for a short time we suffer in the outcome of that decision. However, we have the power of choice available to us at any moment. We have the ability to choose again when something is no longer a fit—as long as we give ourselves permission to.

Sometimes we get stuck and we end up resorting to one of our default coping methods and feeling like we're victims of our own decisions. We are free at any point to begin again. We have the power within us to keep our life aligned to our desires and what feels good.

I knew that if this decision ended up not being a good fit, I would be able to harness my inner CEO and start the steps I've laid out so far in this book. I would assess how things were going, admit when things were fucked, identify where in the Ladder of Self-Worth my rungs got out of order and put them back—reprioritized—in the order they should be in. I would make a new decision based upon the information and beliefs that I had available to me at that very moment, and, lastly, take ownership over that new decision.

With a plan in place, I was ready to look forward with a sense of possibility and wonder to the opportunities that lay ahead—whatever they might be.

PUTTING IT INTO PRACTICE
Step 4: Ownership Creates Opportunity
. . . .

I'd like to start this section by reviewing what we learned in the previous Putting It into Practice sections so that we can use that information in this exercise.

After assessing the health of your enterprise you have an idea of what areas of your human relationships department are going well, and which need some adjustment.

What two subdepartments scored the lowest?

_____

_____

_____

You have learned a new method to help you get unstuck and have learned that admitting that things aren't going as planned is necessary to create new possibilities.

What problem or situation did you identify?

_____

_____

_____

You have activated your self-worth and identified where your current order is on the Ladder of Self-Worth. You now know that there is some reprioritizing that needs to occur for your enterprise to thrive.

Which two rungs need to be reprioritized the most to be in their proper order?

_____

_____

_____

We are at a prime point in this process where we are ready to reclaim our personal power as we begin to harness our inner CEO. In this step you are going to make a new decision—based on the information you have available to you today. Remember, at the end of this step you will be giving yourself permission to choose again. It's not important that this be perfect: it's important that it gets done.

What decision can you make that helps you reclaim your power and supports your being at the helm of your enterprise?

_____

_____

_____

Examples:

I am going to honor myself and say "no" instead of "yes" when I really mean "no."

I am going to use the AWTAF method in real time to break the habit of my old DCM.

I am going to update my résumé and look for a new job.

I am going to start my side hustle and start working toward having my own business.

Now that you have a decision, in the following exercise you'll apply the three steps to owning a decision to help build confidence in your decision-making ability. After all, if you are CEO of your own life you need to have conviction in your decisions so that others follow your lead. If you are wishy-washy someone else may try to harness your energy rather than you harnessing your own.

EXERCISE
The Three Steps to Owning a Decision

....

1. **Stand Behind Your Decision**: Based on your current beliefs and the information you have, list up to four reasons why you made this decision.

   _____

   _____

   _____

2. **Create a Fan Club**: You will need support as you go into new territory. Identify up to three people who support your success, understand you, and will answer the phone or reply to you when you reach out. List your ideal fan club members below:

   _____

   _____

   _____

3. **Permission to Choose Again**: Life is ever-changing and rigidity is a recipe for unhappiness. I have seen many people make a decision and, rather than stand behind it in a self-honoring way as described above, stubbornly stand behind it as it begins to sabotage their life. There is no award given to you for pushing through situations that make you feel small, that are harming you, or that no longer serve you. When you begin to feel out of alignment or like

something is wrong, this is where you can give yourself permission to choose again.

Below: Write a little note to yourself, granting yourself permission to choose again—and as many times as you need to—until your enterprise is thriving.

Dear (First Name) _____,

I grant myself permission to choose again and make new decisions as many times as needed until my enterprise is thriving. I now have a step-by-step system to support me in doing this. I am reclaiming my power and am confident in my ability to make myself a priority.

I am committed to harnessing my inner CEO and creating a life I love to live—

because I am worth it!

And so it is,

_____   _____

Sign Your Name   Date

You can return to the exercise anytime at:

www.beccapowers.com/worksheetshyic

JESSICA

I've never seen anyone take ownership over their decisions the way Jessica does. She's very good about her conviction to her decisions and doesn't get tripped up over the details in between. It's absolutely marvelous to watch Jessica in action.

Back in 2012 Jessica was in a relationship with a man she loved, but she didn't feel the relationship was progressing. She was the breadwinner and things felt superficial between them. The two of them had been together for a couple years with no plans for a wedding in sight. Being in her mid-30s, she was concerned that she wasn't going to be able to have kids if she waited too much longer. As I mentioned, Jessica is a devout Catholic—there was no way she was going to have kids outside of wedlock.

Jessica knew she was meant to be a mom—that was her vision. She leaned on her own fan club and her faith as she agonized over a decision. After an emotional struggle, wondering whether to leave her boyfriend, she was finally able to harness her big brave and have the difficult conversation that would change her life. She broke up with him and asked him to move out. I'm not saying Jessica wasn't upset when she finally did this, but by the time she was ready to have the conversation, she was committed. There was no turning back. She was ready to face the unknown and follow her vision.

Several months after asking her boyfriend to move out, she met the man who became her husband. She knew the moment she first saw him that she was going to marry him—and they hadn't even said "hello" to each other yet. She followed the breadcrumbs that the Universe provided, trusted her intuition, and walked up to this man she'd never spoken to before and said something so bold: "You remind me of my grandfather, in a good way—let's dance!"

Fast forward to today, Jessica is earning $500,000 a year, she is married to her soul mate, and she has two beautiful daughters and a stepson she absolutely adores. Jessica is a beautiful example of how ownership of her decision created opportunity in more than one area of her life.

PART 2
PASSION

I love fire
Just the smell of it makes me happy
I relate to fire
Like my flaming red hair
And that burning passion in my stomach
My sun sign is fire
I have fire tattooed on my neck

Fire make me feel alive
My fire scares others
Maybe that's why I married a fireman
to keep me from burning myself
or burning others
But it didn't work

I was never afraid of my fire
Fire is perceived to bring destruction
I believe fire bares rebirth
So I let it burn wildly

My life became a forest fire
It got burned by my flames
Then fire destroyed it
But it grew more beautiful than before

From the ashes I rose
Fire birthed a new life
I was right about fire

That burning passion is back
Only this time it fuels me
Fire no longer burns me
I burn from the inside out
Bright for all to see

"Fire" by Becca Powers

05 / FINDING YOUR FIRE

> *"The Universe is always listening,*
> *and it always says yes."*
> —Gabby Bernstein[5]

PART 1 RECAP

Before we begin Part 2, I want to bring you back to look at your personal power. During the course of the previous four chapters we walked through how to help you step back into your personal power when you are outside of it. When we started this journey, we knew that some aspects of our life were off and could use some adjustment. We needed to define a process to get back on track to thriving: that's what Part 1 was designed for.

Let's review the four-step process to step back into our power:

- Step One: Assess the Health of Your Enterprise

- Step Two: The Admit When Things are Fucked Method

---

5   Tweet by @GabbyBernstein, November 21, 2017, https://twitter.com/gabbybernstein/status/933001067830435840?lang=en.

- Step Three: Activate Self-Worth

- Step Four: Ownership Creates Opportunity

PART 2 OVERVIEW

Now that you have the steps for getting back your personal power, Part 2 will focus on providing the steps to help you maintain it. Life is going to happen and there will always be ups and downs; our goal is to be prepared. This section is about finding passion, setting boundaries, learning how to deal with the transition period from one state to the other, and redefining beliefs so they support you.

You are in the process of harnessing your inner CEO. This process is similar to a leadership promotion at work: when you're freshly promoted, you're passionate about your role. Your passion fuels others to get excited with you and follow your lead. You'll need to set boundaries because if you don't, you'll end up overextending yourself as you continue to dabble in the responsibilities of your old role while taking on those of your new one.

There can be an awkward transitional period that is sometimes uncomfortable: you might question whether you can really perform this role you signed up for—and the answer is, yes you can! Once you embrace your role, you gain a new perspective. Beliefs you had in your old role no longer serve you. You start to develop new beliefs and concepts that are more supportive. This is what Part 2 is all about. In Chapter 5 you'll start to find your fire and ignite your passion.

FINDING FIRE

Owning my decision had restored my confidence. I was back to viewing FTP Travel as a decision to be proud of. Once again I looked at this experience as an opportunity for growth. I was fascinated by the company's operations and was feeling aligned to my mission mantra: People Before

Profits. In my first couple of months with the company, I was awed by how much they really do consider their employees when making decisions. I experienced this in action during the weekly executive council meetings. I was pleasantly surprised to see how much thought went into making sure the contracted traveling health professionals had a great experience working for the company too. Being on the executive council and seeing behind the scenes of a "Fortune 100 Best Companies to Work For" was proving to be that once in a lifetime opportunity I was hoping it would be.

With renewed energy and excitement, I was eager to see what was possible for me within the walls of FTP Travel and for my life as a whole. I was realizing that leaving Dell was more significant than just leaving a job. I had left the industry I grew up in. I felt as if I left part of my identity behind when I walked out of the door for the last time, similar to a divorce or a serious break up. After my divorce from Jack, I was just Becca. No more Becca & Jack. Now I had left tech. There was no more Tech Becca. Once again I was just Becca. With fewer labels defining me, I started asking myself questions like: "Who am I now? What lights me up and makes me feel excited? What am I passionate about?"

I was ready to find my fire.

A NEW VISION LIST

Feeling the need to find my fire and explore what lights me up, I knew what I needed to do. I needed to make a vision list. I know most people would make a vision board, but being a corporate girl, I like lists, bullet points, and structure to get the creative process going.

Jack and I divorced in 2006. At that time the film *The Secret* was making waves with self-help fanatics—like myself—and it seemed like everyone was making vision boards because of it. The idea of cutting up words and pictures from a magazine sounded fun but also sounded too abstract for me. I don't get the same rush of excitement and wonder from cutting up images as I do when I write down my goals and dreams. I decided I would do it differently and make a vision list.

I made my first vision list in 2006 when I was 27 and titled it, "When I'm 30." It was helpful for me to envision my desires a few years out. It gave that linear part of my brain the chance to believe that there was enough time for these things to possibly come true. A few items on my 2006 vision list were: make six figures a year; become a motivational speaker; go to Hawaii; buy a house again—just to name a few. As a result, I was certified as a public speaker at age 29, broke six-figures at 31, bought a house at 33, and went to Hawaii at 34. The process of writing down my goals and dreams seemed to awaken passion and possibility.

In honoring this space of in-between, I was no longer the old version of myself and wasn't quite the new version of myself either. Work had been going well since I began owning my decision. I was looking toward my future with optimism and—it being the end of December—new year resolutions filled the air in the office. I was inspired to make a new vision list titled, "When I'm 40."

I had some stretch goals on my When I'm 30 vision list that I achieved and shared with you, but I also had lofty ones that I did not accomplish that I wanted to carry over to my new list: to be a *New York Times* best-selling author; to own a million-dollar home on the Florida's intracoastal waterway; to have a vacation home in the mountains; freedom to travel the world—to name a few. Now at the age of 35 I got to fantasize about what life could look like at 40. Some new goals I made for myself were: earn $250,000 a year; go on a retreat or two; give myself permission to create things (my inner artist needed to express herself); go on vacation with my mom's side of the family once a year; join a boat club; get my yoga teacher certification; and write a book.

Breaking away from the narrative for a moment, I'd like to share what I have accomplished since writing that vision list back in 2013. I am now 42. Here are the goals I've checked off my list: earning $250,000+ a year;

going on a few retreats; creating things; vacationing with my mom's side of the family once a year; certification as a kundalini yoga teacher; and I'm writing this book! I don't yet have a boat club membership. Of my loftiest goals, all of them are still pending with the exception of the vacation home in the mountains. We have bought the land! Vacation house to be built in 2022.

2014 STARTS OFF GREAT

In starting 2014 the energy still felt new, inviting, as if creation was serving me in the most wonderful ways. By February I had booked my first retreat at the Omega Center In Rhinebeck, New York. I was going to see Gabby Bernstein—author of *May Cause Miracles*—with my bestie Monica. Not long after I booked that retreat, a local opportunity popped up in Fort Lauderdale: Writing for Your Soul, a writers' workshop, by Hay House Publishing. They were doing a three-day experience in May. I would leave for the retreat in June and I was in awe that I would get to do one workshop in May and another June. Thank you, Universe!

I was so excited about this writers' workshop. They would be going over everything from start to finish: how to write a book, what publishing option fits you best, and how to build a platform. They even had a contest for one of the writers to win an opportunity to be published by Hay House— one my favorites in the biz.

When I saw who was headlining as their author of choice to mentor attendees through the process, I nearly jumped for joy. It was Dr. Wayne Dyer, who for me is like Oprah is for others. His spiritual teachings resonate with me so deeply, especially after my spiritual awakening began in 2006, when I needed to understand Universal law in a practical manner. I couldn't believe I would have an opportunity to see him teach live, in person, for three days. I was off to a pretty good start with my new vision.

I AM

"I AM" are two of the most powerful words you can use to begin a sentence. The important thing is what words you use to finish that sentence. Any time you start a sentence with I am, you are creating what you are and what you want to be."

—Dr. Wayne Dyer[6]

The first day of the writers' workshop finally arrived. With great anticipation for learning everything I could about writing and publishing a book, and getting to hear one of my favorite spiritual teachers speak, I left the house with a sense of wonder. I remember Wayne Dyer walking onto the stage that day back in May 2014, wearing a white shirt that said, simply, I AM. I totally had a fangirl moment. I think I screeched in excitement, and my eyes watered with joy. He proceeded to open up the workshop with this teaching. There were 500 people in that workshop and I happened to sit next to the two most incredible women. The three of us were about the same age and immediately felt connected, as if we'd known each other for years.

We spent three days in the most magical energy I've ever experienced. It was the type of event where you not only learned a ton of practical information, but where you knew something mystical was in the air. I left feeling that the workshop had transformed me from the inside out. I knew on both a physical and metaphysical level that this I AM presence was now part of my being.

Life Hack: Use I AM affirmations in the direction of your dreams.

---

6   Facebook post by Dr. Wayne Dyer, August 2, 2014, https://fr-fr.facebook.com/drwaynedyer/photos/10152580944171030.

I AM WORTHY

During that event there were numerous guest speakers. One of them was Nancy Levin who was the event director for Hay House and had just published her second book. She is also a master coach and poet, and she walked those of us in attendance through a series of writing prompts. My poem "Fire" that opens this section of the book was a result of one of her writing prompts that day.

I remember thinking how lovely Nancy was. She was strong, she was articulate, she was creative, and she was vulnerable. Fast forward to the end of 2019, when I finally picked up her book *Worthy*.[7] The subtitle had to do with your net worth's correlation to your self-worth. What a concept. I had already experienced this through the lessons in my own life and was very curious to read her interpretation. I was equally as curious about where I needed to do some work.

By the time 2019 came around, I had restored my self-worth in many aspects. My life was thriving and I was no longer under constant stress. My debt was nearly paid off, and my husband and I had just built our dream home. With the equity we had from the sale of our previous home we had a very fair mortgage payment. Yet, I was nervous that if I didn't explore my net worth to self-worth equation, I might just find a way to devalue myself and prevent myself from moving forward with my dreams.

All of that being said, I knew that the next step for me was to write this book and that in doing so I would face some of my own biggest fears. After reading her book, I knew that Nancy was the one I needed to work with to bring this dream of writing a book to life. I need accountability to stay focused and keep my pesky destructive unconscious patterns at bay.

I applied to be a client in her one-on-one coaching program. She was everything I hoped for: strong, compassionate, direct, and she held the space

---

7   Nancy Levin, *Worthy: Boost Your Self-Worth to Grow Your Net Worth* (Carlsbad, CA: Hay House, 2016).

for me to move through some aspects of myself where I felt uncomfortable sharing and expressing my story with the world. These were the parts of me that feared rejection, criticism, and judgment—the parts of me that didn't feel safe pursuing my passions. Nancy emulated everything I was already teaching others, but on a more masterful level. With her strong focus on self-worth, boundaries, and self-prioritization, I knew I was in the best hands to complete this level of my transformation into the role of author, speaker, and coach in the public eye.

As I think back to my first encounter with her at that retreat in May 2014, I never in a million years would have thought I would be coaching with Nancy Levin. I never saw myself coaching under any author for that matter, as if something like that was out of my league. That first writers' workshop continues, to this day, to bring miracles into my life. It took a while to fully own it, but I now believe I AM worthy—worthy of actualizing my dreams, worthy of having support in doing so, and worthy of making money doing what I love.

I AM Worthy.

I AM A WRITER

There was another guest speaker at that event who also changed my life. Her name is Tara Robinson, the editor at *Whole Living Journal* and the author of *The Ultimate Risk: Seven Mysteries to Unlock Your Passion and Purpose*—also published by Hay House. That weekend, however, she was not yet a Hay House published author. She had previously done an interview with Wayne Dyer for her radio show and for her magazine, and she wanted to share the experience with the audience. In addition, she offered audience members an opportunity to be published in her magazine. She encouraged us to submit an article and to follow up if we didn't hear back from her.

A couple weeks later, I decided to write a chakra meditation inclusive of an I AM affirmation for each chakra. I wrote the article, submitted it, and heard nothing back. For any non-writers reading this book, this is a pretty common theme when you submit your work: nine times out of ten you don't hear back. I had become pretty used to that. I had no hurt feelings over it.

I did want to take Tara's advice to heart though. I looked at the article, touched it up, and resubmitted it with a follow up note. To my surprise I had an immediate response. The response said that they were very interested in publishing my article and were happy to see me follow up because they had lost sight of it with the number of submissions they received. They accepted it and published it.

Hearing back from the *Whole Living Journal* felt like a dream come true. I was going to have my first article published. I was going back and forth with one of the editors from Tara's team who asked if I had any I AM products that correlated to the meditation I had written. If so, they would be happy to mention it in the article. At that time, I did not. However, I replied, "Of course I do." I immediately jumped onto a T-shirt design website and created a chakra shirt for each I AM statement. I created three samples and had them shipped to my house. I took pictures of them and submitted them with the article. My "Chakraful Expressions," a spiritual clothing line, was born in June 2014 and within a month after the submission, I was a published writer.

I AM a Writer was an I AM statement I could now believe. Thank you, Wayne Dyer, for the magic of that weekend and giving me the gift of one of my biggest dreams, through my own self-realization.

I AM a Writer.

MIRACLES IN RHINEBECK

The time had come for Gabby Bernstein's retreat at Omega Institute in Rhinebeck, New York. I would fly to JFK to be picked up by Monica and her husband. They lived nearby in Highlands, New Jersey. From there we would drive to Rhinebeck.

Monica is a clinical psychologist. She has been to the Omega Institute on several occasions for her training with Dr. Brian Weiss. She often talked about how amazingly peaceful and magical this place is. She had very little knowledge of Gabby Bernstein but she knew I was a big fan. Between her love for Omega and my love for Gabby this retreat was a bucket list item for our duo. Once we arrived at the Omega retreat grounds, I immediately understood why Monica had such a feeling for the place.

Monica has a hidden talent. She is extremely connected with the Earth and all of its animals. Her nickname is Snow White. During this trip she spotted more animals with her bare eye then I could have noticed if I tried. We had so much fun walking around the grounds, feeling stress roll off our shoulders. Reconnecting with the Earth and the air, we remembered that we were much more than the hustle and bustle of our careers, our families, and our commitments. Within the first hour of being there we had made contact with our souls.

After we settled in, we went for another walk. We started with a stop at the bookstore. Both of us are avid readers: the smell of books is something we could totally bond over. I happened to be wearing a bright yellow T-shirt that said "I am Bold"—it was one of the shirts I had made the week before when asked if I had any products.

As we were leaving the store, the buyer asked me, "Is that a chakra shirt? Clever!"

"It is and I made it," I said

"Do you have a T-shirt company?" she asked.

"I certainly do."

"Do you have a catalog?"

"I do but it's at home." Truth be told, I didn't but I knew I could easily make one. I took her card and told her I would follow up with her after the weekend was over.

"Although I do want to see the catalog first, I plan on buying all the chakras!" the woman responded.

Monica and I walked out of the bookstore in full disbelief. We were in complete awe of what had just happened. This was just the beginning—the retreat hadn't even started yet.

WHAT KIND OF YOGA WAS THAT

The retreat started on a Friday night. We were already experiencing miracles and we had only been there for a couple hours. We grabbed our seats for Gabby's opening lecture. Monica and I absorbed her beautiful words and felt ready for a weekend of connecting to ourselves, the Universe, and others.

The following morning Monica and I awoke to the beautiful songs of birds as the sun rose. When we walked out of our cabin, I could smell the pine trees and the grass. The air was clean, thin, and easy to breathe: waking up in itself was refreshing. We left the cabin to hit the cafeteria for some coffee and breakfast. Afterward, we headed to the retreat.

Monica and I are "back of the class" type of girls. We spent all of Saturday and Sunday at the back of the room and were totally okay with that. Gabby opened the retreat with a kundalini yoga set. It was unlike any yoga I had ever experienced. I had been doing yoga since 2006, so by the time I got to Gabby's retreat I had been doing my practice for eight years. My preference was hot yoga. I also did my fair share of hatha and vinyasa classes. But this, I had never done before.

The yoga set did something to my body and soul that I can't quite explain. Something significant shifted that day. After we did the yoga set, she brought us into a savasana: the pose you do after the yoga set. You lie still and allow your body and mind to relax as it integrates all the life force you just gave it.

There was a beautiful live gong. The sound seemed to melt over us and through us as we lay there after our yoga set. Gabby led us in a guided meditation that helped us connect with ourselves on a deeper level, preparing us for the weekend.

I wasn't more than a minute into this experience when the tears began. Tears I didn't know I needed to cry. It almost felt as if some kind of major release was happening on a much more cosmic level and the tears were just an outer expression of that cosmic experience. Lying there on the floor and letting the tears flow, we were guided to look at our sacral chakras.

All chakras are significant, but the sacral chakra is especially so—it is the womb of creation. This is the chakra that births babies, projects, concepts, creativity, music, and all the creative arts. This is the chakra that creates your life. This chakra contains a lot of our mother energy, both as a mother to our children and as a child to our mother. Mommy issues can live in here and stunt your life from its full expression. The sacral chakra is the home to our emotional frequencies ranging the scale from debilitating fear to extreme joy. This is the chakra of passion. Knowing that we were at this retreat to expand our radiance and connect with our true self, as a yogi, I was not surprised that Gabby focused on this chakra.

As I was scanning my body, and my sacral chakra specifically, I noticed something really strange. My sacral chakra, this glowing orange energy ball, was on the outside of my body rather than on the inside of my body.

I remember laying there thinking, "What the heck?" I have learned in the years since that I had deep rooted fear of sharing my creativity, my emotions, and my truth with the world due to mommy issues. It would take me years to learn that I rejected my own light and my own success. This was the first glimpse into the shadow within me that needed the most healing.

THE EIGHT-ARMED GODDESS

In that moment, with little insight as to what seeing my chakra on the outside of me meant, I continued to allow the experience to happen rather than shutting it down with my logical side, which was my initial instinct. Then another incredible visualization happened. Whether it was real or imagined doesn't matter—it was everything I needed.

As I lay there with a sacral chakra outside of my body, just allowing it to be there without trying to fix it, a Hindu deity appeared in my vision. Prior to this vision I had no idea who this deity was by name. I had seen pictures of her randomly over the years at yoga studios or in Indian restaurants. I'm not sure when I might have seen her in passing the first time, but I knew exactly who she was when she showed up.

The deity who revealed herself to me was Kali—also known as Kali Ma or Mother Kali. She has eight arms. Four of the arms are those of a warrior and the other four are those of a goddess. Kali represents duality. She represents death and life. In folklore it is said that when she is seen in a vision it represents death of the ego. It represents the death of one life for the rebirth of another. It's claimed that she either presents herself as a warrior or as the ultimate goddess as she is Mother of the Universe.[8]

In these legends, it's said that when she shows up as a warrior, you can expect devastation and destruction. As legends have it, when she shows up as a warrior it is because you haven't been listening to your calling and your ego needs to be slayed. When she shows up as a goddess she will look beautiful and decorative. You will be able to feel her love and compassion as she encourages you to follow your instincts and step into your true self.

The goddess version of Mother Kali visited me that day. In a weird way, I will admit that I really needed her. Because my mother passed away when I was 22, I have missed very important matriarchal guidance and energy

---

8   Mark Cartwright, "Kali," Ancient History Encyclopedia, June 21, 2013, https://www. ancient.eu/Kali/.

that most women receive from their mothers. It had been 14 years since I had felt that maternal love. When Kali showed up in my vision, she was decadent and absolutely gorgeous, eight arms and all. She felt compassion for me that I didn't have for myself—or even knew I needed for myself. It would take years for me to really understand the message and the magnitude of this experience.

I understand now that I have hidden behind the successes of my career, my coaching programs, kundalini yoga—even championing other people's work that has inspired me. I have been able to use my sphere of influence and belief in other people's work to help my clients harness their careers and lives. I know that I've provided tools that have helped others heal from the inside out.

What I didn't understand until recently is that I wasn't born to hide behind other people's work. I was born to create my own body of work and stand behind that. That takes a whole new level of courage, confidence, and conviction that I didn't know I had—or would ever have for that matter.

That day, I lay there on the floor, sobbing as Mother Kali held me like a mother holds her baby. I felt like I was being rocked and told everything will be okay. After 14 years of not being hugged by my mom, I felt I really needed all eight of her arms to make up for the lost time. Before the visualization and experience ended, Mother Kali gently put her hand on my sacral chakra that was glowing outside my body and made the motion to push it back inside my body. I heard her speak for the first time. She said, "Child, this belongs inside you," and slowly pushed the chakra back into my body. I felt a light shock in my body—like the kind you get from one of those stupid lighter gag gifts.

As soon as the shock hit my body, Mother Kali vanished. The intensity of the experience melted away. Gabby guided us back to awaken from our experience and the gong ceased its cosmic boom.

In the span of just a few months I had found my fire, and that passion was burning in the direction of my dreams.

PUTTING IT INTO PRACTICE

Step Five: Finding Your Fire
. . . .

Awakening possibilities start with creating a vision of macro and micro goals. While macro goals focus on the larger overarching goal, micro goals help us accomplish those macro goals. For example, my macro goal was to write and publish a book. My micro goal was registering for and attending a writers' workshop.

This concept sounds easy on the surface, but it's pretty common for people to struggle doing both. Some people are more visionary and have no problem creating macro goals, but they have a hard time creating and completing micro goals, thus resulting in dreams unfulfilled. Others have a hard time giving themselves permission to dream and often spend cycles in micro goals with no real momentum toward their potential because they lack vision.

I have learned from being an avid dreamer and an action taker that to really harness your inner CEO you need both. I created an equation that has been on a Post-it at my work desk for the last few years. This message serves as a reminder that it takes my macro as well as my micro goals to move in the direction of my dreams.

Vision = Possibility

Action = Probability

Now that we have a little context around macro and micro goals, let's awaken possibility. In the exercise below, you have an opportunity to create three macro goals along with their corresponding micro goals. This is where you can give yourself permission to dream big, go for lofty goals, or even reaffirm a goal you currently have. At the end of your macro and micro goal-setting, you will have a bonus opportunity to turn your goal into an I AM statement. Remember, it's powerful to use I AM in the direction of your dreams.

Here's an example of how to complete the exercise:

- Macro goal: Write a book

- Micro goal: Attend a writers workshop

- I AM statement: I AM a best-selling author

Macro Goal 1: List a macro goal and up to three supporting micro goals below

- Macro: _____

    - Micro: _____

    - Micro: _____

    - Micro: _____

I AM Statement: _____

Macro Goal 1: List a macro goal and up to three supporting micro goals below

- Macro: _____
  _____

    - Micro: _____

    - Micro: _____

    - Micro: _____

I AM Statement: _____

Macro Goal 2: List a macro goal and up to three supporting micro goals below

- Macro: _____
  - Micro: _____
  - Micro: _____
  - Micro: _____

I AM Statement: _____

Macro Goal 3: List a macro goal and up to three supporting micro goals below

- Macro: _____
  - Micro: _____
  - Micro: _____
  - Micro: _____

I AM Statement: _____

EXERCISE

The Vision List

· ·

Feeling passion and desire is an essential turning point in the process of your becoming CEO of your own life. This vision gives you conviction that it is worth pushing through the uncomfortable to create lasting positive change in your life.

Can you imagine a life where your relationships are happy and healthy? A life where you are in the best health of your life? A life where you feel connected to purpose and how you earn money for a living? A life where ease, joy, and abundance are a part of your everyday lifestyle? Can you imagine your life thriving?

I hope you can! This exercise is designed to help you create vision, passion, and desire for a life that you love to live. Here is a reintroduction to the four primary departments in your life:

- Human Relationships

- Health and Wellness

- Profession and Purpose

- Prosperity and Abundance

In the exercise below, write three desired outcomes for each department of your life.

Human Relationships

Example: prioritize myself—deep connections with my kids—a safer and softer relationship with my mom

_____

_____

_____

Health and Wellness

Example: meditate every day—be in the best health of my life—use food as medicine to overcome health issues

_____

_____

_____

Profession and Purpose

Example: start a side hustle—change careers—write a book—prepare for a promotion

_____

_____

_____

Prosperity and Abundance

Example: earn $250,000 a year— go to a tropical island—rent an RV and travel—pay off debt

_____

_____

_____

You can return to the exercise anytime at:

www.beccapowers.com/worksheetshyic

CONNIE

When I thought of choosing an example of awakening possibility, Connie was the first person who came to my mind. Connie is part of a sisterhood of friends I have had for over 20 years. You've already met Monica, and there's Sherri, too. We met in 1997 and have seen each other through multiple relationships, jobs, and hairstyles. We even do an annual girls' trip every year.

Connie is a badass, covered in tattoos. Whether she is rocking a mohawk or a shaved head, she looks amazingly hot and powerful. She embodies fire. She is not afraid to reinvent herself and start something new. As a result, Connie has had many different types of jobs, from 911 dispatcher to school bus driver to business leadership.

I remember sitting in my Durango during a lunch break during my early days at FTP Travel. Connie called me out of the blue. It had probably been a good six months since we'd talked, but as with many dear old friends, we can go months without talking to each other. Yet as soon as we do, it's like no time has lapsed. It's a beautiful thing!

I could hear the stress in her voice. She'd finally had enough of being overworked and undervalued at her job. She was in retail management and they worked her to the bone. The pressure was out of control and she wanted to know if I knew of any jobs she might be a fit for.

I told her I had recently started a new job with FTP travel and that, while I didn't think any manager gigs were available, I thought there was a client executive role that she would be a great fit for. She sent over her résumé and I referred her in. She was an instant fit. They loved her and she loved the company. Just like that, one of my best friends was now working at the same place I was.

We worked together for a little less than three years. She ended up being one of my peers and worked on the client side of the house while I worked on the candidate side. But I have to say, although Connie and I worked at the same place, we had far different experiences. When Connie and I would meet up with Sherri and Monica for our annual trip, Sherri and Monica often said it didn't sound like we worked for the same company.

Connie thrived in that role, but by the time she got to her five-year mark, the long hours were having a toll on her spirit and body. She knew it was time for another round of reinvention and a new vision. Her husband is a veteran and unfortunately suffers from PTSD. For years, the medications prescribed for his symptoms seemed to just make everything worse. Around this time, news of the medical benefits of cannabis were making waves, especially for veterans suffering from PTSD. After much consideration, her husband began to test different strains to see if it helped relieve the symptoms. To everyone's surprise it truly did, and he transitioned from prescription pills to cannabis.

Connie was over the moon to have her husband back. She saw firsthand the power of medical marijuana and wanted to become part of the movement. Shortly after her husband's experience with it, marijuana became medically legal in Florida. Connie had a new vision that was tied to a passion—she wanted to help people heal, the same way she saw her husband heal. She knew that she not only could lead with passion but that she also had the experience to do so. She took the leap of faith and resigned from FTP Travel for a managerial role in the medical marijuana industry.

Soon after getting her feet wet in the industry, she found another role that suited her even better—the general manager role of an up-and-coming organic medical-marijuana farm. She was hired to open their first stores and manage one of them. Soon after opening, they saw rapid expansion and she was promoted to director of retail. The stores are named One Plant and are located throughout Florida with plans for more growth. Connie not only took on the role of opening several stores but also spearheaded opening their call center and their e-commerce site.

As I was writing this book, Connie reached out to Sherri, Monica, and myself via our Facebook Messenger group to let us know she was going to be interviewed by HIGHLIFE Magazine! Fast forward a few weeks and HIGHLIFE Magazine named her Florida Women in Cannabis winner of 2020.[9] She created a new vision for herself that was tied to purpose. She stayed true to herself. She was confident in her talent and abilities and is being paid her worth.

Connie dances with the Universe. She prepares in the direction of her goals and then allows the magic force from behind her and within her to

---

9 "Connie Woolsey: Florida Women In Cannabis Winner 2020," HIGHLIFE Magazine, November 23, 2020, https://highlifemagazine.us/connie-woolsey-florida-women-in-cannabis-winner-2020/.

guide her along. That's what this chapter is all about: dancing with the magic of knowingness within you; knowing that new things and new ways will support you in the most incredible way if you give space for the new to enter when you awaken possibility.

06 / YOUR PERSONAL PERFORMANCE REVIEWS

"Girls you've gotta know when it's time to turn the page."

—Tori Amos[10]

THE DAY THAT EVERYTHING CHANGED

After returning to work from the back-to-back retreats, life was feeling pretty good. In the period of 45 days I had an article published, I unexpectedly started a yoga-inspired T-shirt business, my family was thriving, and I was loving my job.

Then, in one day, it all changed. I remember coming back from a family vacation and being pulled into the office of my sales director on my first day back. I wasn't particularly concerned. I was used to having many closed-door meetings because of my role as a sales leader. We often talked

---

10 Tori Amos, "Northern Lad," written by Tori Amos for *From the Choir Girl Hotel,* 1998.

about sales, performance, and our people. Coming back from vacation I fully expected a debrief.

As I walked into the office of my director, I could sense this was going to be a different conversation. My senior manager was in the room as well. They were both sitting there with the typical, "We're going to have a serious conversation with you" disposition. My mind immediately flew to my team of very vocal and rebellious salespeople and I thought, "Holy crap what did one of my team members do?"

I was shocked when I learned the conversation was about me. I had been a record-breaking sales executive and sales leader my entire career. I had never been pulled into the office for performance—ever. I *had* been pulled into an office for my attitude or for being a sales diva but that's a different story.

I remember thinking, "I've been here less than nine months, I couldn't possibly have screwed up anything that bad." My director said to me, "Becca, I don't know how to say this so I'm just going to try to do my best. I know you're really gung ho to work here and it's clear that you're trying to make an impact but we need you to tone it down a notch. And what I mean by a notch is like 50 percent. I'd like you to think of it as like Becca Lite. Do you think you can do that?"

I didn't know whether to laugh or cry. That statement alone is pretty damn ridiculous. And in all my career years I had never heard anything like it. It goes without saying that I was highly caught off guard. My mind went searching for an answer and I couldn't find one. What they were really saying is I was too much. My effort was too much, my skill was too much, my ideas were too much, and I was making others uncomfortable. I was in shock.

I bet you're wondering how I replied. After all, I am a strong, powerful woman who doesn't like to take any shit. You're probably thinking that I gave this guy a piece of my mind. But I didn't. What he said to me that day struck one of my deepest, darkest trauma scars from my childhood.

THE INITIAL WOUND

I grew up being too much for my mom. I have no intention of painting my mom as the bad guy. She wrestled with her own darkness and did her best to deal with my "too muchness." My mom lived in a constant state of stress and depression. Add some alcohol to it, and there wasn't enough patience for me and all the things I wanted to do and say.

I've been a fighter since the moment I was born. I had the umbilical cord wrapped around my neck three times and almost died. I spent the first couple days of life in NICU and didn't quite get the bonding experience most newborns get with their mom. I was born with fire, passion, and fight. I rebounded quickly from my traumatic birth.

There were moments in my life when I could definitely say that this fighting spirit of mine gave my mom a run for her money. But the trauma wound I'm referring to didn't have to do with my fight—it had to do with my light.

When I was five (and even younger) I was extremely psychic, to the point that I could converse with spirits. There were several times when my gifts scared the crap out of my mom. I totally get it: when your four-year-old is locating lost items with her mind instead of looking for them, it's a little weird. As I trusted my gifts, they got stronger. I started giving my mom messages from the other side. That is when my mom drew the line and told me I was the devil, I was evil, and that there was something seriously wrong with me. I got spanked, set to my room for countless hours, went without meals, and got screamed at and shamed more times than I can count.

Eventually, my mom won. I rejected myself, my gifts, and my light so I could be accepted. I felt very much that if I presented my mom with what she wanted to see, I would win the affection and approval that I so desperately yearned for. To accommodate winning my mom's approval, I only got to express about 50 percent of myself when I was home. Here I am 30 years after that initial wound was opened, being asked again to be 50 percent of myself at work—a place where it was always safe for me to be in my full expression.

ACCEPTING THE UNREASONABLE

I honestly don't know how long I sat silent in that office. It could have been 30 seconds or three minutes. I know that my director and the senior manager had no clue how significant an ask this was for me. As I sat there, spiraling out of control on the inside, I snapped out of my trance on the outside. I knew I had to pull my shit together to get out a response. Words were hard to find. The wound had been ripped back open.

I wish I could tell you that I contemplated saying, "No." In hindsight I wish I had, but then I wouldn't be here writing this book. I had trusted that both managers were in my corner completely. I had a good relationship with both of them. I thought they must be seeing something I wasn't able to. With fear setting in, the last thing I wanted to do was create waves.

While my heart felt like it was beating outside my chest, I stared at them both blankly and said, "Sure, I'll give it my best. Do you have any suggestions for what that would look like?"

My director said, "No more Microsoft Excel. Just spend time with your people."

That response, in that moment, felt like he had come back for a second round of attack.

I said back to him, "No more Excel, are you joking?"

"No," he said. "I think it would be better if you didn't."

How I even made it out of that conversation is beyond me. Looking back now, I'm still unsure how anyone can agree to be 50 percent of themselves. I operate in the land of authenticity, so this agreement I'd made meant that it would require me to not be myself. I had officially accepted the unreasonable. I still find it incredible how one conversation can either empower or destroy. This conversation would be the start of a three-year downward spiral.

I NEEDED MY FAN CLUB

I left work that day and knew I needed a member of my fan club. I knew Jessica was the one I needed to call and went straight to her house. As soon as I saw her, she gave me a hug and I immediately started to cry.

I was defeated. I was lost. I was scared. I was confused. That day I chose to step out of my power and give it to a company simply because it had a motto of Putting People First. In reflection, I valued my personal mission mantra, People Before Profits, more than I valued myself.

Jessica did the best she could to help me get my head on straight and implored me to get the fuck out of there. I remember Jessica saying, "Oh Becca, I'm so sorry. Girl, you don't deserve this. You are Becca Powers. Why don't you just come back to tech."

"I've only been there nine months," I said. "I don't want my résumé to look like I bounce around."

I probably could have given Jessica a million excuses why I was staying at the job. But the real reason was that I was back in my trauma loop and I needed to get their approval and validation. I wasn't going anywhere; I was going to prove to them that I was worth it.

BECCA LITE EMERGES

After getting home from Jessica's house, I was pretty sad. I cried myself to sleep that night and for the following three nights. It was as if my soul knew then that I had just abandoned myself. I could feel myself getting smaller, and it hadn't even been 12 hours yet. Could I go back to tech like Jessica suggested? All my colleagues would surely make fun and call me out. I was in love with my belief of People Before Profits and I just couldn't give up yet.

The next morning I did my best to pretend that everything was okay. I was well-versed in this coping skill. I'm naturally pretty happy and excitable. These two traits get turned up a notch when I'm stepping out of my authenticity. I learned from my childhood that being happy, excitable, and saying "yes" stops the rejection I get for being myself. I just wanted the pain to stop so I turned on the happiness and excitement.

Being a corporate girl, the ask for me to stop using Excel felt particularly vindictive. Regional sales managers are trained in analytics: I have grown up using Excel to understand the performance of my teams. When used correctly it helps with tracking performance, understanding your trends, and being able to move with the market. I know that at some point we've all had Excel-heavy managers who use this tool as a way to tell us about our performance, but I'd like to think that I'm not that type of leader. I do like understanding performance and I do believe that it's absolutely necessary. When you're in sales, there are goals and commissions. I've always wanted the people on my teams to succeed and thrive by meeting their goals and maximizing their commissions. I used Excel to help them reach their potential; having one of my primary tools taken away made me feel like I was flopping in the wind.

On my way to work that day I must have shouted every affirmation I knew to help pull myself out of the darkness that I felt. It helped a little, enough to get me out of the car when I arrived at work. I walked into the office feeling so ashamed and so embarrassed, as if I were defective. I felt like everybody was looking at me. It felt like, in the movies, when the kid walks into the classroom and for no reason everyone starts laughing at him. I felt like everyone knew that there was something wrong with me and that I wasn't fit for this culture and this role.

I wanted to run away and cry, but I sucked it up. I pretended I was okay. I tried my best to say that I understood the feedback and that I was on board with it.

Becca, in the beauty of her fullness, was told to stay home because she was too much. Sadly, Becca Lite showed up and took her place.

> *Life Hack: Don't turn down your light to be lite.*

WOLVES IN SHEEP'S CLOTHING

Because I had accepted being 50 percent of myself, I had a hard time trusting myself. I could no longer tell friend from foe. I started basing decisions about my life and my family on the opinions of others. I believed that others had the best intentions for me. I believed that I could trust the direction of my leadership and my peers to make this job work. But I soon learned that there were also wolves in sheep's clothing.

I was vulnerable, I was weak, and I was prey. The truth was, not many people wanted me there. To put it in perspective, I was the first new hire in over three years. My peers never really liked the fact that I was hired from the outside. The salespeople were also pissed that the executive team hired from the outside rather than promoting from within.

My speculation is that I was asked to tone it down by about 50 percent because it was making the other sales leaders and sales people uncomfortable and the director had received complaints. In typical FTP Travel fashion, they listened to the feedback from their employees and tried to accommodate the best they could. My best guess is that my director and my senior sales manager, who I respected greatly and who I know were happy to have me there, had the best intentions for the organization when they sat me down and asked for me to be Becca Lite.

Walking in that day, I knew that my director and senior manager would be communicating with the other leaders, reporting that they had asked me to turn down my volume. This made me feel very small. Pretty much from that day forward, I stopped participating at the level I was used to. They asked me to mentor under people whose leadership style I did not respect. I felt like they were trying to mold me into someone I wasn't.

It never worked. As small as I felt, I wasn't willing to conform to something I didn't believe in. This caused even more friction for me within my peer team. They would often approach me as if they had my best interest in mind and provide me unsolicited feedback. As a way of protecting myself, I normally responded with a big smile and a nod of approval just to get them to go away. Very rarely did I conform to any of their suggestions. I believe to this day that they were threatened by me and that slowly, over time, they were trying to break me. I felt supported at the leadership level but disrespected at my peer level and was an unaccepted outsider from the sales team.

Looking back, it's hard to believe I let people treat me like that. But I know now that I didn't value myself enough to create boundaries. I trusted people based on their words, rather than picking up on the clues of their actions. I didn't have the courage to evaluate people to ensure they supported my well-being and growth.

I learned from this experience that we do not need to seek approval and validation outside of ourselves. Receiving solicited feedback is one thing but the pure need for approval and validation from others is another. When we adjust who we are for the sake of someone else's approval, it's a clear sign that we just jumped onto the slippery slope of lowering our self-worth.

PUTTING IT INTO PRACTICE
Step 6: Performance Reviews

. . . .

In the previous chapters we spent our time assessing our enterprise and how we prioritize ourselves, identifying how we cope with our problems, how we activate our self-worth, why it's important to take ownership over our decisions and how to tap into passion and desire for our future. This chapter is about other people and how we relate to them and they relate to us.

Typically, the question isn't, "What's the problem?" it's, "Who's the problem?" Once you identify who the problem is, you can then decide whether they deserve a promotion or demotion with the walls of your enterprise. In some cases, you may even need to fire people. It takes a lot of courage to really look at who is truly supporting you, who is supporting you for some type of gain, and who is saying they support you while their actions say otherwise. Let's identify some people, memories, and feelings as they relate to support you've received in the past.

Supportive Experience

I want you to close your eyes for a minute and put your hand over your heart. Take three deep inhales and exhales. I want you to visualize a time when you were truly and genuinely supported.

Example: Someone helped you study for a really hard certification. As a result, you got a promotion. This was true support; the other person had nothing to gain other than seeing you succeed.

I want you to think about your own experience:

Who was it that supported you?

_____

_____

What about this memory makes you feel supported?

_____

_____

_____

What emotions are you feeling and why?

_____

_____

_____

What about this moment helps you feel safe and secure?

_____

_____

_____

Supportive Experience with Gain Attached

I want you to close your eyes for a minute and put your hand over your heart. Take three deep inhales and exhales. I want you to visualize a time when you were supported by someone but their support had something in it for them to gain. This doesn't make the experience bad, it is just to separate the feeling from support with no motive.

Example: Someone helped you study for a really hard certification. As a result, you got a promotion. Your promotion gave them the opportunity for a promotion into your former role.

I want you to think about your own experience:

Who was it that supported you?

_____

_____

_____

What about this memory makes you feel supported and what about this memory did the other person have to gain?

_____

_____

_____

What emotions are you feeling and why?

_____

_____

_____

What about this moment helps you feel safe and secure? Does anything about this memory have you questioning their intent?

_____

_____

_____

Unsupported: When Words and Actions Don't Match

I want you to close your eyes for a minute and put your hand over your heart. Take three deep inhales and exhales. I want you to visualize a time when you were not supported. Perhaps someone said they would support you but their actions told you otherwise.

Example: You were studying for a certificate that you needed for a promotion. Your boss says they support you but their actions tell you otherwise. During this precious study time, your boss gives you an increased workload making it impossible to have time to study. As a result, you failed the certification and did not qualify for the promotion.

I want you to think about your own experience:

Who was it that was not supporting you?

_____

_____

_____

What about this memory makes you feel unsupported and what in this memory did the other person have to gain by not supporting you?

_____

_____

_____

What emotions are you feeling and why?

_____

_____

_____

What about this moment makes you feel insecure and not safe? Does anything about this memory have you questioning their intent?

_____

_____

_____

Now that you have gone through and identified what support looks like in its varying degrees, you can take a deep breath. On the exhale say the word "clear" and shake your hands out. This will help you reset.

EXERCISE

Performance Reviews: Top Five Daily Influencers

. . . .

In this exercise we are going to begin a performance review on the top five influencers in your life. This a symbolic performance review. It's designed to help you gain clarity around the people you interact with the most, to help you determine whether they are friend or foe. It's not on you to offer everyone an explanation as you choose to promote or demote the sphere of influence you allow them to have. You don't owe the ones that are holding you back that sort of time or energy.

The people in the exercise will range from family to coworkers to bosses to friends. The goal is to identify the people who truly support you and are committed to seeing you succeed as well as identifying who are haters and have the possibility to bring you down. Remember, people can be wolves in sheep's clothing. Because of that, I'm going to provide a list of yes or no questions to help you score the top five influencers.

For a final round of clarity, we are looking for the five people who impact your decision making, and influence how you go through life. These might be the people you are trying to impress or over-validate your actions to, or they might be people you genuinely trust and who are a positive force in your life.

Using an example from this chapter. My top five influencers were: my director, my senior manager, my husband, Monica, and Jessica. If you are unsure who your top five are, look at your phone. Who were the last 10 or so people you texted with? Good chance you will find a few there.

PERFORMANCE REVIEWS: TOP FIVE INFLUENCERS AND THEIR SCORES

There are five yes and no questions to run each influencer through. It's important to answer these based upon their actual words and actions, and not on what you hope their words and actions are. The results will be in the form of a score. The higher the score, the more supportive they are. The lower the score, the less supportive they are.

Score Index: Y=1, N=0

1. Name:

    - Does this influencer embrace your talents and gifts?

    - Does this influencer give you the respect of their full presence?

    - Does this influencer provide you with support and room to grow?

    - Does this influencer want you to succeed?

    - Does this influencer suggest that you choose their needs over yours?

Performance Review Score: _____

Based upon their score, do they deserve a promotion or demotion?

---

2. Name:

    - Does this influencer embrace your talents and gifts?

    - Does this influencer give you the respect of their full presence?

    - Does this influencer provide you with support and room to grow?

    - Does this influencer want you to succeed?

- Does this influencer suggest that you choose their needs over yours?

Performance Review Score: _____

Based upon their score, do they deserve a promotion or demotion?

_____

3. Name:

- Does this influencer embrace your talents and gifts?

- Does this influencer give you the respect of their full presence?

- Does this influencer provide you with support and room to grow?

- Does this influencer want you to succeed?

- Does this influencer suggest that you choose their needs over yours?

Performance Review Score: _____

Based upon their score, do they deserve a promotion or demotion?

_____

4. Name:

- Does this influencer embrace your talents and gifts?

- Does this influencer give you the respect of their full presence?

- Does this influencer provide you with support and room to grow?

- Does this influencer want you to succeed?

- Does this influencer suggest that you choose their needs over yours?

Performance Review Score: _____

Based upon their score, do they deserve a promotion or demotion?

_____

5. Name:

    • Does this influencer embrace your talents and gifts?

    • Does this influencer give you the respect of their full presence?

    • Does this influencer provide you with support and room to grow?

    • Does this influencer want you to succeed?

    • Does this influencer suggest that you choose their needs over yours?

Performance Review Score: _____

Based upon their score, do they deserve a promotion or demotion?

_____

After completing this exercise, let's do a quick reflection:

Who from your list scored the highest?

_____

Who from your list scored the lowest?

_____

What was your biggest takeaway from this exercise?

_____

_____

_____

You can return to the exercise anytime at: https://www.beccapowers.com/worksheetshyic

CARMELA

Carmela is one of my clients. She is an entrepreneur and extremely talented in the field of holistic health. She is an organic aesthetician and has the most soothing private office for her clients to relax in as she brings their skin to new life. She is a certified holistic nutritionist as well as a certified yoga teacher. She brings all of these modalities together to be a rock star holistic health coach.

I first met Carmela five years ago in a certification program. When we met, she was working as an aesthetician at an organic spa. Her boss at the time undervalued and underpaid her. This had Carmela fuming. She was the lead aesthetician and the lead in sales. The thing that made Carmela upset was that she got such a small percentage of her sales compared to neighboring spas. Having signed a non-compete, she was unable to leave her spa and work at any of the others without penalty. She tried desperately to get her boss to comply with her requests for a higher percentage of sales but it was to no avail. Eventually, Carmela got to a point where she needed to put her boss through a performance review. When she realized she wasn't going to be able to make that job work, she embraced her big brave and made the ultimate move to get out of her non-compete: she opened her own aesthetician practice.

Carmela, aspiring to get her business into the six figures, often was brought down by the dynamics of her relationships, whether personal, romantic, or work-related. She had a childhood past of dysfunction like so many of us. The unfortunate part of her story was that her unconscious attachment to dysfunctional relationships had kept her from living a life she deserved.

As a business owner, she had much more responsibility on her plate. She was now responsible for all the aspects of the business: marketing, sales, services, etc. She was nervous that she wouldn't be able to build a successful practice. But with the talent and reputation she had, she felt confident that she would be able to do well and pushed past the fear. She did well until that pesky pattern of being tangled in dysfunction reared its ugly head again. She found herself romantically involved with a partner who didn't make her a priority. He was one foot in and one foot out. The uncertainty of the relationship pulled her focus away from her business as she focused instead on trying to make the relationship work. Ultimately, he got a performance review and she realized he wasn't going to be able to give her what she needed. Carmela ended up parting ways with that relationship when she realized it didn't serve her. She again put her focus on business.

With her business beginning to thrive again, Carmela was feeling good. Then dysfunction found her again. It was as if every time she felt good, she attracted a situation that would cause disarray. This time it would be even worse. Carmela ended up falling in love with a man who had narcissistic traits and who loved to drink. Of course this was not how he presented himself. By the time she figured out what was going on, she was already living with him. This is where our paths crossed again and she hired me to be her coach. She knew that my program helped women find empowerment and break free from the limitations that hold them back from living their best life. It was going to take a Herculean effort to get out of this relationship and she needed support. Because her business was barely getting any of her attention as she spun in the web of her partner's narcissism, her sales had dropped. Her daily energy was extremely low as she felt she was constantly walking on eggshells. It was time for Carmela to do another performance review—knowing what the outcome would be.

While Carmela was good at performance reviews, she wasn't as skilled at seeing when danger was coming. This was rooted in her childhood. Her nervous system thought dysfunction felt safe. It was a very outdated program that was controlling her life. As a result of going through all the steps

I share in this book, Carmela has now harnessed her inner CEO. She is no longer attracted to dysfunction. She is standing in her power at the helm of her enterprise, focusing on nurturing herself and growing her business to six figures. As I was writing Carmela's story in this book, she had just purchased her dream car—a Jeep Wrangler—a vehicle she had held off on purchasing because of financial or relational limitations. You can now find her smiling ear to ear with the windows down, Wrangler top off, and the wind blowing her hair.

07 / THE BRIDGE OF IN-BETWEEN

"She understood that the hardest times in life to go through were when you transitioning from one version of yourself to another."

—Sarah Addison Allen[11]

A TRIP DOWN *WHAT IF LANE*

It was July 2014 when I was asked to be Becca Lite. I suddenly became fearful that I would lose my job. The need to survive kicked in. I made the decision that day that I would do whatever it took to make the job work. I couldn't run the risk of leaving my family vulnerable without income. I was the primary breadwinner. I would sacrifice whatever I needed to.

I started to trip down *What If Lane.* I began to ask myself questions like:

- *What if* I didn't comply with this ridiculous request to tone it down?

---

11 Sarah Addison Allen, *Lost Lake: A Novel* (New York, NY: St. Martin's Press, 2014).

- *What if* I quit and the tech industry wouldn't hire me back?

- *What if* I didn't comply, lost my job, and I couldn't pay the bills?

- *What if* I was a fraud and really wasn't good at being a regional sales manager?

- *What if* they were right and I was too much?

The further I tripped down *What If Lane* the more disempowered I became. I began saying "yes" when I meant "no." I started working long hours to prove that I was willing to put the job before my family. I was constantly asking for feedback in a search to understand if I was complying with the Becca Lite request. As a result, I became less and less of myself. As I became less and less of myself, my emotional unavailability increased for the people I cared about the most—including my kids.

 ## HELMET CHECK
Decision Breakdown

It's time to pull away from the storyline to do another helmet check. Let's break down this decision of mine to do whatever it took to make the job work and reframe it with my self-worth intact. If I were to face making a decision as to whether or not I was going to comply with the request to be Becca Lite today, I would confidently choose not to comply. Instead of deciding that I needed to do whatever it took to make the job work, I would make the decision that I needed to do whatever it took to preserve my wholeness and dignity.

Standing with my self-worth intact, my trip down *What If Lane* would look more like this:

- *What if* I sacrificed my self-worth to comply, how would that impact me?

- *What if* I believed that something was wrong with me, what would that do to my self-esteem?

- *What if* I lowered my standards to match theirs, who would I become?

- *What if* I stood up for myself and told them that is not something I could ever do, how would that empower me?

- *What if* I owned my value and recognized that they don't, how would that help me stay whole?

As I go through this reframe, I know that if I had asked these questions I would never have allowed fear to take over. I would have stood up for myself and spoken my truth that this was not something I was willing to do. I would have honored my worth and began to search for another job.

Before we get back to the story, I'd like to share a lesson with you that I've learned. Anyone asking you to tone it down and adjust yourself—whether it's in your professional or personal life—does not have your well-being as a priority, they have theirs. It's not your responsibility to make someone else's life feel better by adjusting yourself to fit their comfort or expectation level. It is your responsibility to make your life feel better by considering your needs before someone else's—this is true self-care.

THINGS GOT WORSE BEFORE THEY GOT BETTER

Getting back to the story, it was October 2014 when I got the next wave of news that would shake my foundation. This would be the phone call that my dad passed away. As I mentioned in Chapter 2, he was my hero, my protector, and my voice of reason when things got tough. Having lost my mom back in 2002, I knew that this was going to be a devastating blow. I immediately put myself in grief counseling. Losing my dad on top of stepping out of my authenticity, made me feel like there was a CAT-5 hurricane living in my body. The emotion was so intense at times that it would literally bring me to my knees and leave me short of breath.

I felt for my husband and kids because I felt powerless, broken, and confused. I had unintentionally handed my husband the reins for raising all four kids. He did the best he could, but he lacked a mother's touch. My husband is an everyday hero. He goes out and saves lives every third day and then comes home to be a husband and a dad. My husband's grandfather, PopPop, had a very heavy hand in raising him. PopPop was former military and was a cop in Miami during the 1950s when the Rat Pack was hanging around. He had a very structured, old-school way of raising kids. Following suit in the regimented life, my husband has been a firefighter paramedic since he was 18 years old. The military-structure approach to raising kids had worked for PopPop, and my husband and his two kids from his first marriage were used to it, but it was enough to send shock waves through the nervous systems of both of my kids.

It still pains me as a mother to reflect and know that my emotional availability lacked a strong presence for two and a half years—time I will never get back. My daughter, Tyler, and my son, Braydon, were not prepared for the stylistic change in parenting. Having been raised by hippies, I have a much more tender, compassionate, and understanding approach toward how I raise kids. Jermey and I compliment each other well, and balance out our parenting styles. He adds the structure, which the kids do thrive in, and I add more compassion and understanding to help them move through life. When either one of us is in the lead for too long, with four kids, things get a little crazy.

My kids specifically suffered immensely from my accidental emotional abandonment. Like I said, I was there, but I wasn't there. If you have experienced something similar in your past or are experiencing something similar now, the best thing you can do is wake up from the illusion that you are powerless. Even though I wish I could turn back time and remove the impact my emotional unavailability had on my kids, I am very aware that I can't.

What I *can* do is acknowledge where I was and how it impacted them, make my amends, and build a bridge to the future. During that time, which our entire family now refers to as the dark years, the pressure that I inadvertently put on Jermey to raise our kids while I was at work 12 hours a day, nearly broke our marriage.

Although his style of parenting caused major distress in my kids, I was unable to really see it because I was in my own state of extreme distress. Instead of realizing that I overloaded him and the kids, I thought he was purposely being mean to my kids. With both my husband and my kids stressed, I felt like I was in the middle of a war I didn't want to be in. Do I choose my kids? Do I choose my husband? The answer was neither. I needed to choose myself—so that I could choose them.

> *Life Hack: Choose yourself first so you can fully be there for others.*

ANOTHER CLOSED DOOR MEETING

Fast forward to October 2016. By then I had spent two years in this state of extreme distress. I know that I have painted FTP Travel to be the bad guy and the root cause for my pain and suffering. In many ways it was. But for many others at FTP, it was the best company to work for and the best job they'd ever had. I had desperately wanted that to be my reality. Despite the mixed feelings about working there, I really believed in their mission of putting people first. As a leadership team we were constantly doing tons of events, programs, and gifts for our employees. Being a part of the executive council really did give me an experience of a lifetime. But for me personally, the bad outweighed the good.

Needing a break from the stress, I took some time off and went on vacation with the family. By the time I took this vacation, I had put on 30 pounds, formed two anxiety disorders that required medication, and I was living under chronic stress. I had hit my emotional rock bottom and was starting to put myself back together piece by piece. I finally had had enough. I was getting my Becca back and growing more and more impatient with my job and how I felt they treated me.

I don't know what it is about going on vacations while I was with FTP Travel but every time I returned from one, I felt like the rug was pulled from under me. This would prove to be no different. Returning from vacation, I was pulled into another closed-door meeting. However, this time I was no longer the scared five-year-old begging for acceptance. I was a grown-ass woman who had been through hell and back and wasn't about to tolerate another round of puppeteering and manipulation.

Here I was, in the same position as I was in July 2014 when they ripped open my initial wound. I was about to get told some untruth so I would conform. I was really close with my new senior manager and my director, who had recently been promoted from senior manager and I could tell they were highly uncomfortable with the conversation they were about to have with me. I braced for it. I knew whatever they were about to say wasn't going to be good.

I FINALLY GOT PISSED

It felt like I sat there in silence for an eternity before the silence was broken. They proceeded to tell me that a manager from another part of the organization was transferring to our team. They told me who it was, and I thought it was a good choice. Following that statement is what shocked me. They went on to tell me that my rookie recruiter of the year, who I had trained, no longer wanted to be on my team.

The recruiter on my team felt I wasn't strong enough and wanted to go to the new manager's team. I didn't buy it, not even for a minute. Even if parts of it were true, I have seen the level of manipulation that goes on to get employees to do what the business needs them to do. It was typical to influence the employee to think it's their idea. I was always disgusted by this but was no longer surprised. By this point, I had been with the company for three years and had seen it all.

I remember them asking me how I felt about it, but I knew they didn't really want to know. If I had expressed the deep rage that had been festering inside me for two and a half years, I would have directed all of that hurt, anger, and disrespect right at them. On the other hand, I knew they were just fulfilling a task. It was not their own doing. This decision had come from executive leadership. I knew my senior manager and director wanted to hear that I was okay with it so that they could do what they were going to do anyway, with all the ends neatly tied up. So I said, "Okay, do what you need to do."

Then they asked, "Are you really okay with this?"

I responded, "Not really, but it doesn't matter." I remember the look of confusion on their faces when I didn't try to smooth their path, when I didn't try to figure out what was wrong with me so that their storyline made sense. I was sick and tired of something always being wrong with me and I knew I didn't deserve it. I was now aware that a tactic they used was meant to make me feel like I was defective so they could get what they wanted. I wasn't falling for it this time. I knew I wasn't defective, and I finally got pissed.

I went home that night and did what I typically did when things like this happened: I cried. But this time was different. I wasn't crying because I wanted to be understood. I wasn't crying because I wanted to be validated. And I wasn't crying because I wanted approval. I was crying because I was angry. I was crying because I wanted out. I was crying because I finally had enough guts to stand up for myself and it felt good.

I found myself making the epic move so often portrayed in heroine tales when they hit that final moment of defeat right before their rise. I dropped to my knees in the bathroom just like Liz Gilbert did in her book *Eat, Pray,*

Love.[12] I made a deal with the Universe. I told the Universe that if It got me out of this hell, I would faithfully follow Its lead. I promised to take care of myself and never let things spiral out of control like this again.

AN ANGEL IN MY FAN CLUB

The following morning on the way to work, I called Jessica and told her what had happened. I felt like we traveled back in time to two and a half years earlier when I was sitting on her couch crying. I think she said verbatim what she told me then: "Oh Becca I'm so sorry. You don't deserve that shit. Fuck them. Are you ready to come back to tech yet?"

This time, I said, "Yes." When I made my contract with the Universe to follow Its lead and to always take care of myself, I made the commitment to follow the breadcrumbs that the Universe put in front of me. The Universe is always conspiring to support us in the most magical ways if we let go and allow. When I was finally able to assess the situation and admit things were fucked, I invited in possibility. Adding Jessica to the mix meant a miracle was bound to happen.

By the end of the day, Jessica had teed up an interview for me, to go back to Dell. She said, "I couldn't find any regional sales manager roles that are open but there is an outside executive sales position open with a Dell exclusive reseller, vTechio, that I think would be a really good fit for you. I know the owner, and I gave you a recommendation. He'd like you to give him a call." I was in awe of how fast the Universe conspired to support me. A bridge was being built from the world I was living in to the new one I was creating. I was now going to the in-between.

---

12 Elizabeth Gilbert, *Eat, Pray, Love: One Woman's Search for Everything Across Italy, India, and Indonesia* (New York, NY: Riverhead Books, 2007).

STANDING ON THE BRIDGE OF IN-BETWEEN

The in-between is an interesting place to be. It's filled with more mixed emotions than I expected. While I was empowered and excited about my future and what awaited me in this new world, there was also fear around how things would work out. Questions like, "Am I really making the right decision?" often crossed my mind. As I stood in the middle of my Bridge of In-Between, I found myself mourning aspects of what I was walking away from. This was part of my life and I needed to give myself permission to grieve what I'd been through, what I wished was better, and the parts of it I loved. Sadness didn't mean I had to turn back, sadness was an indicator that I was feeling again—I was emotionally present for the first time in a long time. I understood that it was necessary for me to feel my feelings, and keep walking forward.

PUTTING IT INTO PRACTICE
Step Seven: The Bridge of In-Between
. . . .

From our work in the previous chapters, we have a good idea of what our current problem is, and who is at the forefront of the problem. Now we will start building your Bridge of In-Between by starting with a trip down *What If Lane*. First we are going to restate the problem and who is involved in it so that it's here at the forefront before we start our journey down *What If Lane*.

What is your identified problem?

_____

_____

_____

Who is at the forefront of this problem?

_____

_____

_____

How have you contributed to staying stuck in this problem?

_____

_____

_____

What If

What if you sacrificed your self-worth to stay stuck in this problem, how would that impact you?

_____

_____

_____

What if you believed that something was wrong with you, what would that do to your self-esteem?

_____

_____

_____

What if you lowered your standards to match theirs, who would you become?

_____

_____

What if you stood up for yourself and told them that is not something you can continue to do, how would that empower you?

_____

_____

_____

What if you owned your value and recognized that they didn't, how would that help you stay whole?

_____

_____

_____

Now that you have some reframing and are starting to feel more empowered, let's take a moment to reflect on the Bridge of In-Between in the upcoming exercise.

EXERCISE

Standing on the Bridge of In-Between

. . . .

Failure to feel is a common mistake within the world of personal development. With so much focus on wishful thinking, positive affirmations, and manifesting, emotional bypassing often occurs. Now, as you have seen throughout this book, I love all those things, but not honoring our range of emotions is a form of self-rejection that in turn is a form of self-harm. The goal is to honor and heal—not to reject and harm. It's okay to be sad about moving on and excited to be moving forward at the same time. The power of AND is so liberating and freeing. We will get more into that in the next chapter.

For now, I want you to honor all the emotions that come up from this exercise. I'd like you to pretend that no emotion is negative, and give yourself permission to feel your feelings without judgment. Your emotions need you to be a loving mother to them. As one of my dear friends says, "There's so much transformation in the magical messy middle," and that's exactly where we are going.

I want you to imagine that you are standing in the middle of your Bridge of In-Between. When you look backward you see the world you have been living in, and when you look forward, you see the world awaiting your discovery.

Looking Back

Looking backward, what emotions come up as you gain the courage to walk away? Do you feel sadness, grief, anger, relief, joy, or a combo of all of these? What are you feeling as you look back and why?

_____

_____

_____

Looking Forward

Looking forward, what emotions come up as you gain the courage to walk toward the unknown new world that awaits? Do you feel anxious, nervous, excited, hopeful, happy, or a combo of all of these? What are you feeling as you look forward and why?

_____

_____

_____

What emotions need your love and nurturing to keep you walking forward?

_____

_____

_____

What emotions need your strength and perseverance to keep you walking forward?

_____

_____

_____

You can return to the exercise anytime at

www.beccapowers.com/worksheetshyic

| RACHEL

Rachel is another one of my coaching clients. The cool part about sharing Rachel's story with you is that I was also able to bring her through a 13-week program that followed the very steps in this book in their sequential order. Rachel successfully completed the 13 weeks and is now harnessing her inner CEO. This chapter was a really big step in her transformation.

She had been living on her own for about two months before we connected. Rachel was in the process of separating from her husband. She had gotten to the point in her relationship where she felt she was constantly walking on eggshells. She said she had tried to express her concerns to her husband and what she needed from him to feel supported and loved. She felt like no matter how many conversations they had, her pleas all went unheard.

Rachel finally hit her bottom of exhaustion, anxiety, and stress. She gathered up the courage to move out and to focus on herself before making any significant decisions. She was in the space between the old world and the new world, without a system to see her through such a significant transition. We had worked together previously. I had been her direct manager. She was thrilled to find out that I relaunched my coaching business. I told her about my book and all the thoughts that went behind the order of these steps. I felt they would really help give her guardrails as she processed a wide range of emotions.

We started with the assessment in Chapter 1. Her results indicated the HR department needed a morale boost. She felt that. Once we got to Chapter 3, we were able to walk through her Ladder of Self-Worth. I could relate to her results as she mirrored where I used to be: the Universe, others, self. I knew that if we didn't get her Ladder of Self-Worth turned around, her stress and anxiety could lead to further issues.

We were able to get her Ladder of Self-Worth aligned to support her greater health and wellness. Being a people pleaser, she really needed the reframe. By the time we started working on a new vision, Rachel was having a spiritual awakening and was in the process of becoming a new version of herself. She found it super easy to awaken possibility and create a new vision for Rachel Enterprises.

As we entered week six and we started to discuss whether any of the top five or so people that she interacts with had been acting differently in any way. Rachel said, "I didn't really think about it until you asked, but, yeah, things have been different with a few of them." I explained that as she grows and transforms into new desires and a new way of being, it was going to change the dynamics in her relationships. I shared that this happened to me at FTP Travel as I evolved, and I did a quantum leap after attending those two retreats. Although no one could put their finger on it at the time, my energy was vibrating in the frequency of I AM and I was expanding. At work, I found that a lot of my coworkers found this shift uncomfortable and would often try to bring me back down to their level.

I highlighted to Rachel that in order for her to remain in her elevated state and continue to grow, she needed to give the top five influencers in her life a performance review. She laughed at first, but as we went through each person, she realized that shifts were indeed happening.

For an example, a person on her list who she was really close to seemed to be backing off the friendship a little bit. This friend was much more surface level in their conversations than normal. Rachel said the person actually seemed a little jealous or concerned over the new energy she was radiating, as if Rachel—being separated from her husband—should be in a constant state of depression.

Rachel was bothered by this. I wanted to make sure that she felt she had permission to feel the sadness and feelings of betrayal. As a people pleaser, Rachel often stuffs her feelings down to make sure everyone else's needs are met first. I went on to explain that part of the magic of standing on the Bridge of In-Between is allowing you to feel your feelings and validate them as real.

We spend so much wasted time seeking validation from the outside rather than from our inside. In the process of seeking validation from others we invalidate ourselves. This invalidating makes us feel empty, alone, and ashamed, so much so that the feeling part of the process is often bypassed. Feeling your feelings is by far one of the most important parts of rebuilding an enterprise that thrives.

Rachel was in both shock and awe at this process. She stood tall on her Bridge of In-Between and allowed herself to honor the emotions of her past. She felt the love, the guilt, the sadness, and the anger of how things played out in her marriage. For the first time, she gave herself permission to feel polarizing emotions, and that was liberating. Rachel was no longer criticizing herself for feeling mixed emotions. As she looked forward to the future from her vantage point on the Bridge of In-Between, she felt empowered. The mixed emotions of excitement, fear, happiness, and uncertainty were allowed a place within her. As a result, she became more of herself. She became clear as to what best serves her.

Rachel and her husband have decided to move forward with divorce. Standing on the Bridge of In-Between, she now has direction from the clarity and confidence she gained. She feels a renewed sense of self-worth as she was able to feel the wisdom her emotions provided her when she gave them a space to have a voice.

08 / THE POWER OF AND

"I refuse to allow someone to put me in anyone's box."

—Beyoncé[13]

THE MAGIC CARPET RIDE THAT CHANGED MY LIFE

For this chapter we are going to rewind the timeline to a year prior to the closed door meeting you read about in the last chapter. This chapter starts in the summer of 2015 and will end where the last chapter left off, October 2016.

There were times during the dark years when I didn't care about living. I say that because in true purgatorial fashion, I didn't want to die either. This space of in-between left me in a state of non-action and I was stuck. I loved my life and the people in it. The serious thought of truly ending my life never happened, but living was simply so hard. Because I believe we

---

13 Mesfin Fekadu, "Beyoncé talks surprise album, success at NYC event," AP News, December 21, 2013, https://apnews.com/article/3ed4eb3a531a44ff9a3c61d77b4dc75d.

are souls, I fantasized that death might be liberating from all the pain and suffering in this human body. Fortunately, I didn't stay in that darkness for too long, the light found me.

I had come back from vacation in the summer of 2015 and Rachel, who I spoke of in the last chapter, had left a packet of kundalini teacher–certification info and registration forms on my desk. It was placed on my keyboard with a Post-it note that said, "I think you are meant to do this. :), Rachel"

An instant "Yes!" registered in my body—I knew without a doubt I had to do this, she was right. The light within me was trying to break through and I knew it. I just needed to run it by my husband to make sure he was cool with the schedule that would require me to be gone every third weekend for nine months. He supported my decision and I registered.

I studied under Deva Kaur, a first-generation student of Yogi Bhajan. Deva eventually became my mentor in the areas of yogic lifestyle and all things under Universal law, but seeing her for the first time scared me. She was tall, regal, and reminded me of a queen. She was older, like a mother, if I had to guess, she was probably in her early 60s. I'd never thought about it until I sat down to write this, but Deva's energy is very similar to Mother Kali's: an equal balance of firmness and compassion. It makes me laugh now but I spent the first year or so being afraid of her.

I remember the first day of my kundalini teacher training when Deva explained that this process takes nine months. She went on to say, "That is how long it takes to give birth to a human life, and how long it will take for your rebirth." I remember being so nervous and so scared at the same time. It sounded like I was about to embark on some magic carpet ride that would change my life. That is indeed what happened. Kundalini teacher training would prove to be an epic adventure of transformation from the inside out.

AN INNER CONFLICT AROSE

To bring the timeline back into perspective, this nine-month-long teacher training started in October 2015, approximately one year after my dad died and one year prior to getting called back into the office for another closed-door meeting. The more inner work I did, the more my outer world felt constricting. I was beginning to feel like the world didn't accept duality. That you either had to be this "or" that. There didn't seem to be much space to be this "and" that.

Here I was, this corporate sales executive badass and a devoted yogi. I was committed to both my spiritual path and my career—even in the state of misery I was in, my career never left my sights. I remember folks within the yoga teacher–training class telling me I needed to leave my corporate gig to dedicate my life to being a yoga teacher. They would say things like: corporate America is evil and the root of so many problems in the country; that corporate America sucks the soul out of people; that there is no way I'd be able to continue that line of work once I was fully awakened on this path.

Likewise, folks at the office were very perplexed that I was getting certified as a kundalini yoga teacher. They were concerned for me as if I had lost my mind. They would say things to me like: yoga teachers don't make any money—you should really think about things before you give up your day job; or yoga teachers don't live in reality, they live in some fairytale land and have no clue how the real world works. Are you really interested in losing touch with reality?

The thought of giving up my day job to be a full-time yogi *had* crossed my mind a time or two, but I had no intention of leaving my corporate gig to be a yoga teacher. I liked being in sales way too much. The challenge of solving a customer's problem, the fast-paced environment, the adrenaline, the rush of a win, the unification of teamwork—and the money—filled my soul much more than it depleted it. I also very much enjoyed the mindset of being a yogi. Yogis have a tendency to question everything and form their own opinions based on their experiences. They are freedom thinkers who pull away from mainstream stereotypes and conformity; this I loved and fully planned to embrace. And yes, I would love to lose touch with the inaccuracies in reality pushed down on me by others.

This duality created an inner conflict for me. When this is all done, would I become a full-time yogi or would I stay a corporate sales executive? Still deep in my dark years, this was a decision I would have to table.

BREAKING THEIR RULES

The deeper I got into my training, the more I realized how limiting the stereotypes were on both sides. Relieving myself from the pressure of doing anything other than enjoying my teacher-training experience and focusing on my healing, I decided to run my life in parallel, and compartmentalize my two worlds—my corporate world and my spiritual world. I was still trying to make things work at FTP Travel and didn't want to jeopardize anything. The leadership at FTP Travel was definitely of the opinion that hobbies or side hustles outside of FTP Travel were a bad thing. They wanted complete and utter commitment to them and only them. Anything not FTP Travel–focused was seen as a threat—especially if you were in leadership—or maybe it was just me. Maybe I was the threat.

I remember the moment that proved this viewpoint to be true, and I proceeded with caution ever after. It was November 2014—one month after my dad died. I had been accepted as a vendor at *Yoga Journal Live*. I was ecstatic that my chakra shirts were attracting attention. They were selling at the Omega Retreat Center, and now I was vending at *Yoga Journal Live*. I had taken a day off work to accommodate the event schedule. I was posting all over my Facebook for people to come down to the show. I was working the event with my daughter, Tyler, and my best friend, Monica. I was feeling pure joy to be with loved ones, connected to a community I loved, and selling my creations for others to enjoy. I was happy and it showed.

I returned to work the following Monday to be pulled into a closed-door meeting—again—by my senior manager. Apparently I had offended the executive leadership by taking a day off to manage my own business. I was told that it didn't look good to the employees and that, in the future, they would encourage me not to take a day off to promote my own business. This was followed by the politically correct corporate statement, "Of course we can't tell you how to use your PTO, but since it caused some concern it's something you should keep in mind."

I wanted to crawl out of my skin. I was only in the beginning stages of my dark years and my natural reaction to most things was to comply, but even so, this seemed utterly ridiculous to my eyes. I replied, "My T-shirt business is a form of self-expression, similar to a painter selling their paintings. It's my art and I have a right to self-expression and I have the right to sell it. I'm sorry but I feel that the recommendation you're sharing is crossing the line."

I don't think my response landed well with the executive leadership because their actions told me so. In one executive council meeting, the then president said aloud, "If any employees have a side business, they need to make sure they keep it private and that it doesn't interfere with their work." I knew they were referring to me. I was furious. I knew that I had wolves in sheep's clothing on my Facebook page because I never promoted it at work—only on my private Facebook page.

I decided that I was going to break their rules and continue my self-expression, continue to create chakra- and yoga-inspired T-shirts, and continue to sell them. I made the decision to be corporate employed and have a side hustle. My job was trying to force me into an "or" situation: work here or have your T-shirt business, but don't do both. I broke their rule. I said, "I will work here *and* I will have my T-shirt business." I learned then that the "and" made me feel empowered and strong while the "or" made me feel disempowered and small.

In early 2015 I was nominated and selected for the 2015 "50 Women of Distinction Award." These are 50 women professionals recognized for their career efforts and contributions to the community. My role at FTP was highlighted along with my strong belief in putting people before profits. The cherry on top of this was that they also worked my chakra T-shirt business into the article, and along with my headshot, there was a photo of my chakra shirts front and center. I boldly stood in my "and" statement.

FTP Travel was less than impressed and had no desire to circulate this achievement within the organization. I, on the other hand, raised my arms in a V for victory yet again. My lowered self-worth had just gotten a turbo boost.

THE AND SET ME FREE

The power of AND had a similar effect on me as the message, "You are the CEO of your own life," that I received from Markeith, my former VP of sales at Dell. Let me explain: the impact and the empowerment of AND didn't last very long. It joined "You are the CEO of your own life," lying in the background of my mind rather than the foreground until October 2016 when I finally got pissed. Once pissed, I was ready to harness my inner CEO. This was my life and it was my responsibility to get it back on track.

There I was, standing on the Bridge of In-Between ready to harness my inner CEO. I looked back at where I was and then looked forward to where I was going. I started to feel that inner conflict arise. I was feeling sad about walking away. I remember thinking, "What is wrong with me?" I started to feel guilty and ashamed that I felt sad about leaving a place that tried so desperately to control me, and that, ultimately, I allowed it to do so. When I looked forward to where I was going, I felt empowered and proud that I stood up for myself. I had negatively judged myself for feeling sad and heartbroken about a place that made me feel so much pain. Then I remembered the power of AND.

As I stood there reflecting on the past and the future, a rush of empowerment melted over me. It was as if someone had turned on a light switch. I went from a downward spiral of thoughts relating to my past, to a complete acceptance in my present. Once that light switched on, all judgment ceased. I allowed myself to feel sadness, shame, guilt, and anger as I looked back at the past. I also allowed myself to look to the future with awe, optimism, hope, and faith. That's a minimum of eight emotions I allowed myself to feel at the same time. I relaxed into this. I felt the tension in my body melt away. Something miraculous was shifting inside—I had just received a huge shift in perception. The result: freedom!

In that moment, I felt myself processing many AND statements that would support me moving forward on my journey. Here are a few examples of me breaking free from OR and embracing the power of AND.

- I am a sales executive badass and I am spiritual as hell.

- I am super successful and really happy at the same time.

- I am a good mom and I work full-time.

- I work full-time and I am an entrepreneur

These AND statements sound simple, but if they were that simple to embrace, we wouldn't struggle so much with our authenticity. Society, as well as those we surround ourselves with, are so focused on the OR that it causes separation in ourselves. That internal riff causes us to see imperfection where imperfection doesn't exist. It causes us to feel limitations where limitation doesn't exist. It causes us to feel stuck where freedom exists. The power of AND set me free. It allowed me to accept myself exactly where I was: messy and magnificent at the same time.

Life Hack: Replace your "ors" with "and."

PUTTING IT INTO PRACTICE
Step Eight: The Power of AND

. . . .

We are going to start this section by breaking some rules. I mentioned in an earlier chapter that I love structure, but rules?—not so much. And the rules I'm talking about are the ones put on us by society, a job, or a relationship. These rules are not facts, they are suggestions for conformity and control that lead to forms of limitation, playing small, and inauthenticity. They typically have a "this or that" feel to them. Put another way, they often look like, if I'm *this* then I can't be t*hat*.

Let's play a quick game of This or That to see what rules in your life need to be broken. I'll provide a few examples to get you thinking of rules in your own life that are currently holding you back. As you step into the helm of your enterprise, you will need to create your own set of rules.

Examples of Society Limitations:

- If you are curvy, then you're not pretty.

- If you're a mom and you work full-time, then you won't be a good mom

Examples of Job Limitations

- If you make a lot of money, then you're sacrificing your happiness.

- If you are employed, then you shouldn't have a side hustle.

Examples of Relationship Limitations

- If you follow your dreams and become an artist, then you will break your father's heart.

- If you speak your mind, then you're disrespecting someone else and will silently suffer as a result.

Example of Personal Limitations

- If I take care of my needs first, then I am being selfish.

- If I prioritize myself first, then it will take away from someone else.

Now it's your turn. Let's identify five limitations that are holding you back and are ready for some rule breaking!

List five This or That limitations below:

_____

_____

_____

_____

_____

EXERCISE

The Power of AND

. . . .

Now that we have identified some areas that have had you in a state of this or that, we get to use the power of AND to empower us to move forward with confidence and clarity. Truly embracing the AND is a liberating experience and will position you well as CEO of your own life. Below, I'll re-share the AND examples I used earlier in the chapter, then you will create your own AND statements.

Examples from the chapter:

- I am a sales executive badass, and I am spiritual as hell.

- I am a yogi, and I earn six figures.

- I am a good mom, and I work full-time.

- I work full-time, and I am an entrepreneur.

- I am hurting, and I am healing.

Create five AND statements: Take your five *this or that* statements about issues that have caused inner conflict, and put an "and" between them. We are busting through the constriction of stereotypes so that you can be free to be who you are, unapologetically. There are no rules here other than to turn the "or" into an "and." Have some fun here!

Below write five new AND statements:

_____

_____

_____

_____

_____

After writing your AND statements, write down how you are feeling about the experience:

_____

_____

_____

_____

_____

Did anything about the exercise surprise you? If so, what was it that you found surprising?

_____

_____

_____

_____

_____

You can return to the exercise anytime at: https://www.beccapowers.com/worksheetshyic

VANESSA

Vanessa is a powerhouse and a queen—not in some conceited or egotistical way, but in a way that inspires and produces awe. Vanessa and I were both in our late 20s when we met at a women's group called Women's Prosperity Network (WPN), here in South Florida 12 years ago. We were both careered and successful and we were introduced by one of the founders of the women's group. She knew that we would benefit from getting to know each other.

Vanessa and I became instant friends. When we met, neither of us was in a role that supported the magnitude and depth of our abilities. Vanessa knew she wasn't cut out for a traditional corporate life; I remember the day back in 2008 when she told me she was meant to be a C-Level for her own enterprise. I felt the truth in her conviction and I remember her asking me what I was meant to do. I told her I was meant to be an author, a speaker, and a coach. I've seen this vision for myself since I was a kid.

I was growing bitter toward my corporate America gig just as Vanessa was hers. I was in a leadership role that I despised due to the micromanagement that went on at every level. As we both got to share our experiences, we realized we were kindred spirits.

I don't know what happened that day, but we created an unspoken agreement to support each other in reaching our dreams. We talked at least once a week on our rides to work for close to three years. We cried together in our frustration at not expressing our truths in our roles, we encouraged each other to try different roles that got us closer to our dreams, and we talked about manifesting the life we really wanted.

Vanessa was one of the original people who encouraged me to open my coaching practice back in 2008. I remember her saying, "There are no rules saying you can't. Just take on clients that you have the capacity for—one, two, or three clients is still better than none." That had never dawned on me because I was living in an "or" world. I had the misperception that I had to leave corporate America in order to follow my dreams. Vanessa showed me that I can do both and do both well. It was another moment where the Power of AND offered me empowerment, but it was too early in my career for me to recognize it as a tool to get me unstuck.

Vanessa was destined to be her own boss, but, as for most people, her path was a little bumpy. She had been in the cruise industry since college and knew everything about it. She's a gifted leader, salesperson, and marketer, and was highly desired in her industry. She was trying to start her own business, but also made a lot of money in her corporate role.

A couple years into our friendship, Vanessa became pregnant with her first child and decided she needed to have a steady job. She got a marketing leadership role within the industry and, at first, was happy. The role offered stability and she felt she'd have enough freedom to do what she does best. But after some time in the role, the suppression that Vanessa had felt in earlier corporate gigs began to resurface. She knew she was sacrificing her dream: her beliefs about who she was and where she wanted to go were not in alignment with what she was doing. The thought of being a new mom and joining a startup made her nervous. She was feeling the pressure of societal limitations: if she were to join a startup, it would make her a bad mom because she needed to earn a good income.

After giving the corporate gig chance after chance to work out, Vanessa decided to take a huge leap of faith and create her own AND statement. She would join the startup *and* be a good mom.

Vanessa would go on to co-found an organization that helps cruise planners and travel agents have direction, inspiration, and successful sales and marketing plans to implement in their businesses. But to make that happen, she needed to risk it all. Although scared, Vanessa knew this was the opportunity she had been waiting for.

With the support of her husband, they moved from South Florida to North Carolina. In the beginning, the business consisted of just Vanessa and her cofounder, Meredith. They worked their butts off to start up the business, and not only to start it up, but to make sure it would be the powerhouse of an organization that it was meant to be.

Vanessa had a vision of global impact. She had a governing policy not to have her talents and abilities suppressed by others—she broke the rules. Life often offers you a path of ups and downs and sideway trails before you unite with the vision that you hold for yourself. The thing is, you have to hold that vision unwaveringly until you meet it.

Today Vanessa's business is exactly that. She is standing in the expression of the truth she knew back in 2008. She is co-founder and chief sales officer of Gifted Travel Network. They host seminars, conferences, and workshops around the world in some of the most luxurious hotel properties and locations. You can now find Vanessa glammed up on stage, standing in her power, influencing the lives of thousands.

09/

SET BOUNDARIES, BREAK OLD PATTERNS, AND CREATE NEW POLICIES

*"Your freedom lies just beyond
the first boundary you set!"*
— Nancy Levin[14]

THE GIFT OF PRESENCE

Standing up for myself that day back in October 2016 was the first time—in a long time—that I had started to feel like myself again. With all the kundalini training and the deepening of my spiritual practice, things started to shift at a rapid pace. Within a 24-hour period, I had admitted things were fucked, gave the Universe permission to do Its thing, received

---

14 Nancy Levin, "Getting Zen About Boundaries," NancyLevin.com, https://nancylevin. com/getting-zen-about-boundaries/.

a new job lead, and activated my self-worth. I was making significant progress in the direction of harnessing my inner CEO.

As I followed the steps I've shared with you in this book, it became clear to me that I was already whole and complete—I did not need to be altered. After living in a mindset that I had to fix myself to be acceptable to others, this was certainly liberating. Tolerating someone else telling me there was something wrong with me wasn't going to happen anymore. I no longer had to go down the rabbit hole and explore all the terrible things that were wrong with me. Just because some broken person called out one of my flaws, I was supposed to sit and sob? Absolutely not. If I was to be CEO of my own life, it was time for me to develop new policies that supported who I was becoming and where I was going.

I started to feel that my chronic willingness to reflect on and pore over all my flaws was a weakness—a weakness I also recognized in other modern-day self-help junkies like myself. I have learned that too much reflection over a concentrated amount of time can make you feel damaged beyond repair. It can lower your sense of self-worth and make you forget the essence of your magnificence. Narcissists, ego-maniacs, and the threatened will try to point out your every flaw and try to make it look like they are helping you—as if you're the one who's defective and they are some superior being gifted enough to see your flaws and help you fix them. Narcissistic abuse can show up in more than just romantic relationships. It can come from a boss, a coworker, or it could even be in the culture of an organization. If you're in this chronic self-reflection state, there is a high chance you'll take the bait. But you don't have to. Instead, you can pause before reacting, then choose not to accept their criticism and fake help.

Remember you are a queen or king underneath all the messy exterior. Fix your crown, then walk over to someone else and fix theirs. Remember you are unlimited in your potential and that you deserve to shine and sparkle just as everyone else does. No one has the right to make you feel less than. This is why it's important to explore your current beliefs—aka policies— and create new ones from this place of remembering your greatness.

Having not taken the bait from that closed door meeting, I left work that day feeling proud and powerful, renewed in the essence of who I really was—unlimited. I went home from work that night, smiling ear to ear. I could see the relief on my family's face that I was genuinely smiling. They could see the light shining from my eyes. I hadn't even said anything. My husband immediately greeted me with a hug. My kids were excited to tell me about their day and everything they'd learned. I was over the moon that I was finally able to be fully present and hear everything they had to say. The gift of presence had been restored in my life.

THE GRINCH EFFECT

I haven't mentioned it earlier, but I had established a solid meditation practice that consisted of about 15 minutes a day. Every morning before I started my day, I would meditate for 11 minutes, read a passage from a book that inspired me, and take a few moments to journal about it. I do this practice religiously to this day. I have learned that miracles occur in the commitment to the practice, not in the perfection of the practice.

I bring this up because eventually you will have your breakthrough. I was in the dark years for almost three years. I don't imagine you will have to stay in your discomfort for nearly as long. I had a very significant childhood trauma wound that needed validation and approval as protection from people who rejected me. It was almost as if I, as little Becca, felt safe in an environment where I was rejected because I knew how to survive there. As screwed up as it sounds, it felt normal and my nervous system knew how to respond to it.

But life isn't about surviving, it's about thriving, and my soul knew it. My meditation practice gave me the platform to guide myself to a different and much more supportive way to live. It was a place where I could contemplate which beliefs no longer supported me, and which beliefs would help my enterprise thrive.

I remember how I felt the following morning after I made my deal with the Universe. I felt a surge of radiant energy that I hadn't felt in years. I did my meditation, grabbed *A Course in Miracles,* and randomly flipped it open. I landed in the teacher's manual; I believe it's the second or third exercise. In summary, it says that every moment is a gift.[15] That struck me in the most profound way. It meant that my sitting there on my meditation pillow was a gift from the Universe. The 15 minutes that I carved out every day to connect with my soul was a gift. Reading a passage that inspired me was a gift. Standing up after my practice with my two feet on the ground was a gift. Hearing the birds chirp when I stepped outside was a gift. The magnitude of this realization was refreshingly overwhelming and is still alive within me today.

For the rest of that day I was super aware that every moment I experienced was a gift. It reminded me of a story: toward the end of *How the Grinch Stole Christmas!,* little Cindy Lou Who gives the Grinch the gift of love and acceptance.[16] In return, The Grinch's heart grew three sizes that day, and I felt like that was happening to me. I felt extreme gratitude in every cell in my body. It felt as if my heart grew three sizes that day—just like the Grinch's. I call it the Grinch Effect.

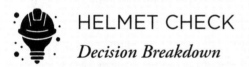 ## HELMET CHECK
Decision Breakdown

There are moments for everything. Including when to or when not to embrace the concept that every moment is a gift. I don't believe that every moment is a gift. I believe some moments are horrific, tragic, and painful and leave a mark on our hearts and our souls. I believe we need to honor the painful moments in our personal story just as much as we honor the joyful ones. The rejection of experiences and labeling them something oth-

---

15 Helen Schucman, *A Course in Miracles* (Omaha, NE: Course in Miracles Society, 2009)

16 Dr. Seuss, *How the Grinch Stole Christmas!* (New York, NY: Random House, 1975).

er than what they are is a form of self-rejection and disconnection from authenticity. From my experience, it causes more disconnection, delusion, and disempowerment.

After honoring the pain in our stories, there is that delicate period where we either go deeper into the darkness or we rise into light again. This is where discernment is needed to determine if it's time to flip the script and rise out of our pain. In my case, it was time to do exactly that. It was time to expand, break free from my trauma cycle, and see every moment as a gift—as an opportunity to rise.

FRESH EYES

This shift in perception reminded me of the day that I saw Marianne Williamson at a retreat at Omega and she dropped a one-liner that pierced my soul. She said, "A miracle is simply a shift in perspective." Now this is a subtle statement that can just fly past you. Thankfully, I caught it. It explained the moment I had on my meditation pillow the morning I felt the Grinch Effect. I had received a miracle. The miracle didn't arrive as some sort of outer tangible—as if I had been praying for a new job or more money. The miracle came in the form of a shift in perspective that allowed me to see every moment as a gift. It also allowed me to see myself as a gift.

On my drive to work the morning of my breakthrough meditation—the same drive I had been doing for many years—I noticed things that I had never noticed before. I noticed big gorgeous trees blooming with flowers in yellows, purples, and reds lining the road, as if to decorate it with their beauty. I remember thinking that I couldn't recall seeing that much color on my way to work before—it was really remarkable!

I noticed other things as well, like the way that sunlight came through the treetops in just the right way for a magical glimmer. I remember thinking, has that always been there?

The drive was 30 minutes. I normally used the time to either shout affirmations or to talk to one of my girlfriends. On this day, however, I chose simply to listen to the radio and enjoy the drive. I had a lot of pop music stations programmed in my car because I had preteen girls, and one of their stations played in the background while I experienced the newness of this drive.

I was about five minutes away from work when I heard a song called "Fresh Eyes" by Andy Grammer. It had been released in the summer of 2016 and by October it had gotten some pretty regular airplay on the radio. My daughter, Tyler, particularly loved this song. I will never forget the impact the song lyrics had on me.

"So suddenly I'm in love with a stranger, I can't believe she's mine, now all I see is you with fresh eyes."[17]

I felt like my higher self or divine self—whatever you want to call it—was singing directly to me. As I intently listened to the lyrics, I began to tear at the truth they revealed to me. By seeing myself as a gift, I had given myself permission to fall in love with myself, my new self, and I can't believe she's mine. She doesn't belong to anyone else, she's mine now to love, protect, and to care for. I can look at myself with fresh eyes.

Before I got out of the car, I knew it was time to protect my shine and my sparkle. I believed I was worth it. I believed I had the right not to have something wrong with me. I believed it was time to create a boundary that would guard my tender heart from any more chronic self-reflection.

THE BOUNDARY BETWEEN ME AND ME

I walked into work that day ready to develop new policies for myself. What that meant for me was that it was time to take a look at my beliefs and reframe the ones that were rooted in limitation and my playing small

---

17 Andy Grammer, "Fresh Eyes," written by Andry Grammer, Ross Golan, and Ian Kirkpatrick for *The Good Parts*, 2017.

for other people. It was also time to set some long overdue boundaries. With the power of AND—and a set of fresh eyes—I knew I was in a place where I could reframe, create new beliefs that supported me, and set boundaries with people I had previously allowed to walk all over me.

Starting with boundaries, that morning I committed to myself that if any decision required me to lessen myself in order to accommodate the incoming request, the answer would be "no." It was one boundary, but it was a good one. The agreement I made was with myself, not with anyone else. I would learn much later from my coach, Nancy Levin, that the reason that boundary became so powerful was because I made it with myself. She shared with me that without proper boundary training, we often try to set boundaries between us and other people. The problem with that is that you can't control other people. When you make the boundary between you and yourself, that is where you can become a boundary badass. For a deep dive on boundary setting, read Nancy Levin's book, *Setting Boundaries Will Set You Free*.

Exercising this new boundary would prove to create more tension than I had anticipated. Let me explain: At work I was known as the "yes person." If anyone in leadership asked me to do anything I generally had one of these responses—yes, sure, no problem, I'll do it—no matter how it made me feel about myself. Setting my new boundary between me and me changed the dance. My director no longer knew what to do with me and my new stances of, "No, perhaps you should ask someone else," or "My plate is too full, I can't," responses. This new dance was awkward for me, too, yet wildly empowering.

As a result, I found myself being included in fewer meetings; more responsibilities were being passed to other people. Although I made this choice and it was the right choice, my inner control freak was freaking out. I began to feel excluded and undervalued. The people pleaser in me wanted to say "just kidding" so that I could be liked and accepted. I knew, however, this was a losing strategy and I had to keep the commitment of saying "no," if saying "yes" made me feel less than or kept me in a position of playing small. I told myself it was better to be uncomfortable and say "no" than to sacrifice my well-being to say "yes." This ended up being a winning strategy.

> Life Hack: It's better to be uncomfortable and say "no" than to sacrifice your well-being to say "yes."

OLD BELIEFS ARE STUBBORN

A lot of things were going great for me: I had a new boundary that was helping me break the toxic tie between me and FTP Travel. I had a new belief that I was a gift and worthy of protecting. The fresh energy I felt was bringing in new opportunities. Jessica's referral to the Dell exclusive partner seemed more and more like a fit. A month had passed since that last closed-door meeting at FTP Travel, and I was less involved with the business than I had ever been before. I even felt disconnected from my team and extended teams. Even so, guilt was creeping in; I knew I would have an offer soon and if the offer came in, it would blow my current earnings out of the water.

But old beliefs are stubborn. I had deep-rooted beliefs that to be whole, I needed to be accepted and validated by others. Quitting would give the opposite response. I would be rejected and possibly be asked to leave immediately. My nervous system was again taking a hit. In an attempt to avoid the pain of rejection, I asked myself what the minimum raise was that I needed to stay at FTP Travel. I definitely needed a raise as I was having a hard time making ends meet after three years of reduced salary. The answer, I decided, was $10,000. Before the offer came in from the Dell exclusive partner, I wanted to give FTP Travel a chance to keep me.

I tapped into my big brave and asked my senior manager and my director for a $10,000 raise. Shortly afterward I was told, "Not at this time," which was followed by all the things I needed to fix in order to "one day" get a raise. I had been there for three years and had never had a raise, I knew "one day" didn't exist. The moment I heard this information, I felt as if I'd been slapped out of my old self and was back into the new version of me that was emerging. I felt disappointed in myself for slipping backward. Then I remembered that my stubborn old beliefs were so deeply rooted in my childhood that I need to give myself permission to choose again. I paused for a moment, acknowledged what I was being told, and in that moment chose that I was worth more than this job could ever offer me.

Just a few weeks later, right before Thanksgiving 2016, I had an offer from the Dell exclusive partner for $175,000, exceeding what I was making at FTP Travel by a third. I was so happy; it was the start of reclaiming my value. It's worth mentioning that in order to get the offer I had to have a reference from Dell. And who did the owner of vTechio want to call? Calum, my former sales director, that I skip-leveled my resignation to. I nearly wanted to barf from the level of discomfort I was feeling at the sheer thought of calling him and asking him for a favor. I am so grateful now that I worked things out with him back then, and had given Dell a month's notice. Despite my previous feelings on how he managed his team, he really came through for me and gave me an excellent recommendation. I learned an important lesson: *never burn a bridge on your way out—you may need to access it every now and then.*

I waited until after the Thanksgiving holiday to submit my resignation to the leadership at FTP Travel. The resignation was emotional because I had to confront the part of me that thrived on their acceptance and validation. I resigned with the request that they not try to counter-offer or ask me to stay. I had made my decision to leave and I was asking that it be respected. I was trembling as I took this stance. This was new for me as I was still in my wound. This time they complied with my request rather than my complying with theirs. I said I would be happy to stay through the end of the year. My last day at FTP travel was Christmas Eve.

Those stubborn old beliefs had just had a reality check; I was the one in charge and the old beliefs knew it. Ever since, they've never tried to hijack my self-worth like that again.

 # HELMET CHECK:
Decision Breakdown

We're going to pull away from the story timeline for another helmet check. I made a decision that supported me and I want to use that example to show how you can shift into beliefs and boundaries that support you. Ultimately, you can develop new policies that help your enterprise thrive.

We are going to start by looking at how to deconstruct stubborn old beliefs. First comes identifying the pattern that is no longer serving you. In the example I provided in this chapter, I had a long history of needing validation and acceptance to feel like I was worthy. I sought these things outside of myself until it caused so much pain that I was forced to reconsider whether it served me any longer.

Next, I created three pattern check-in areas that I could use to help me break free from the grip of my old belief.

- **Actions**: What did my actions and behaviors look like when this belief was running the show?

- **Limitations**: What limitations do I put on myself as a result of allowing this belief to dictate my actions?

- **Emotions**: What emotions do I feel when I do this?

And, finally, I got as close to the core of that old stubborn belief as I could. I looked at the pattern and the answers to my pattern check-in to understand what was going on. I then tried to be concise and clear as to what this old stubborn pattern could be. I have found that the simpler the answer, the more successful I am in getting out of its grip.

For this decision breakdown, here are all the answers I came up with:

Identify the Pattern: I seek approval and validation from others to feel worthy.

Pattern Check-In:

- Actions: What did my actions and behaviors look like when this belief was running the show?

    - When making a decision I sought someone else's advice.

    - I stayed loyal to the point of harming my well-being to prove my commitment.

    - I leaned into my default coping method and powered through, hoping things would work out.

- Limitations: What limitations did I put on myself as a result of allowing this belief to dictate my actions?

    - I was not doing what I know is good for me. I was doing what others thought is good for me.

    - I lowered my value by not honoring what I need.

    - I lost empowerment by not making my own decisions.

- Emotions: What emotions did I feel when I did this?

    - Loss of control

    - Fear of rejection

    - Indecision and confusion

OLD STUBBORN BELIEF: I AM NOT WORTHY

That old stubborn belief was hard to digest but I knew it was running the show. It wasn't hard to see the need to develop a new policy. I was able to lean into the new perceptions that had trickled in, especially the perceptions that I was a gift and so was my life. This gave me confidence to stand in a new, more empowering belief: I am worthy.

Embracing this new belief—I am worthy—was an essential step in building new policies, beliefs, and boundaries that supported the thriving enterprise I was in the process of building.

PUTTING IT INTO PRACTICE
Step Nine: Policies That Empower

. . . .

Let's start to develop policies that support you building your thriving enterprise. Following the process above, we'll work on debunking an old stubborn belief and replacing it with a new empowering one. You can go to https://www.beccapowers.com/worksheetshyic to download this worksheet for as many old stubborn beliefs as you want to work on. Here, we will only focus on one. It's time to get real with yourself, and you have plenty of material to pull from the previous chapter. I want to see you harness your inner CEO and live your best life! To do that we need to debunk the oldest most stubborn belief you have.

Now that you have more clarity as to what and who the problems are in your life, what pattern in yourself do you recognize as part of the problem?

Identify the Pattern:

Example: I seek approval and validation from others to feel worthy.

_____

_____

Pattern Check-In: List up to three for each check-in point.

- Actions: What did my actions and behaviors look like when this belief was running the show?

Example: I stayed loyal to the point of harming my well-being to prove my commitment.

_____

_____

_____

- Limitations: What limitations did I put on myself as a result of allowing this belief to dictate my actions?

  Example: I was not doing what I know is good for me. I was doing what others thought were good for me.

  _____

  _____

  _____

- Emotions: What emotions did I feel when I did this?

  Example: Loss of control

  _____

  _____

  _____

After reviewing all of the above, try to get to the core of your old stubborn belief in seven words or less.

Old Stubborn Belief:

Example: I am not worthy.

_____

_____

How did you feel after getting to the essence of an old stubborn belief? What insight do you have now that you didn't have before?

_____

_____

We saved the fun for last. Now create a new belief that empowers you, a belief that will serve as a new policy as you harness your inner CEO.

My new, more empowering belief is:

_____

_____

EXERCISE
One Big Bad Boundary

· ·

As we move into this exercise and continue to develop policies that em-power, you are required to create—at minimum—one big bad boundary that you are willing to put in place between you and you. As I shared earlier in the chapter, this was a game-changer for me. I didn't know at the time but this is the proper way to set boundaries and that's why it worked so well. Knowing this information now is going to set you on the right path for staying at the helm of your enterprise. The truth is, you can't control anyone else, but you *can* control how you react. Setting this boundary will help you do that.

Question: If you had the chance to create one big bad boundary what would it be?

Ponder that as we get started on the exercise.

Below, you are going to create a boundary that empowers you, protects your previous energy, and prevents you from doing things for others at the expense of yourself. Here is my example from earlier in the chapter: *If any decision required me to lessen myself to accommodate the incoming request, the answer would be "no."*

Perhaps yours will look more like:

If my husband picks a fight, I'm going to choose to walk away peacefully and read a book.

If my boss asks me to stay late, I will say "no."

I will pause before I say "yes" to something to see if I really mean yes or no, then say "no" if it's a no.

Write your one big bad boundary here:

_____

_____

_____

You can return to the exercise anytime at: https://www.beccapowers. com/worksheetshyic

ERICA

Back in April 2009 when Jermey and I were first dating, he invited me to meet his friend Matt—a fellow firefighter—and Matt's wife, Erica, along with their two kids. Erica and I were instant friends. I saw qualities in her that I really adored. She was smart, she was funny, and I could tell she was just a good person.

I learned later that Erica was a graduate of the University of Florida with a bachelor's degree in public relations. She had spent some time doing fundraising for the American Cancer Society but left when she and Matt started a family. When I met Erica, her daughter was just six months old.

Matt was also a firefighter and worked with Jermey. Matt and Erica were living off one income and you could tell they were just barely making ends meet.

As time went on, my friendship with Erica grew and we began talking about careers. She loved being a stay-at-home mom, but she also missed working and using her talents. I saw her as a mentee, she saw me as a mentor, and I wanted to guide her to her career. It seemed as if her talents and capabilities were shining through her—they were so obvious to me!

I remember sitting at her dining room table in 2009 when she asked me what I did for a living. I explained I was in tech sales and that I earned a little over $100,000 a year doing it. She was in complete awe. She asked what type of degree I had, and I said with a smirk and a laugh, "No degree—I'm a three-time college dropout." She looked at me as if I was magical and had accomplished the impossible: earning six figures without a degree.

I looked Erica in the eyes and said, "I have been in sales since I was 18 and have been doing this for a long time." I was just 30 years old at the time but I still had over a decade of commissioned sales experience.

"I only wish I could do something like that," she said.

"Why can't you?"

Erica shared a list of reasons why she thought she couldn't. I told her that I could refer her into the company. We had an entry level position that started at $65,000 a year with a four-year degree from a major university.

"I have that!" she exclaimed excitedly.

"I know!" I said with equal enthusiasm.

We started talking more about her applying. She was beginning to see how transitioning would benefit not only the family but her needs as well, yet she was also facing old stubborn beliefs that didn't support her. She didn't believe she was worth it. She challenged me as to why they would hire a stay-at-home mom who hadn't worked in a couple of years. I challenged her back: "Because you are amazing and we would be lucky to have someone with your smarts and drive."

As we discussed it more, I could see her energy begin to shift from possibility to conviction. We went through the financial impact it would have on her family. I felt confident that Erica would excel in the position and get to a higher paid position quickly. Erica was willing to adapt to a new, more empowering belief that she was worthy of the role.

I started talking about the chakras and how our root chakra is about safety and security. When activated and balanced, it activates our personal power. She said, "If you get me this interview, I'm going to wear my red power shirt."

We both laughed. "You've got a deal," I agreed.

Erica was eventually brought into the interview process. On the day of the interview she showed up in a pantsuit with a red dress shirt. I still remember how authentically powerful she looked. During the interview, they asked her the standard barrage of questions. But when asked if she felt comfortable selling software she replied, "Yes, I am. I had a portion of my career where I had to sell 'hope' for a living. If I can do that, I can learn to sell software." The hiring managers seemed to agree, and she was offered a position right then and there.

Erica and I were overjoyed at her ability to put herself and her courage first. After three years of being a stay-at-home mom, she was now employed and about to wow the world with her talent. She ended up being one the fastest promotions in the company's history, receiving two promotions—from sales lead to account manager—within a year. She started the year at $65,000 and ended the year at $100,000.

Erica is now earning over $200,000 a year as an enterprise account executive, and all because she was willing to develop new policies that empowered her. Her big bad boundary that she has maintained since that day is: I am willing to bet on myself first, before I bet on anyone else.

PART 3

PROSPERITY

Money doesn't grow on trees
I was told
You just need to make enough to survive
I was told
Money doesn't define you
I was told
I should be modest
I was told

If I fantasized about having more
I was told I'll never achieve it
If I wished for more
I was told I was wasting my time

Money felt like a thing that I wasn't supposed to have
Or should be ashamed for having if I had too much

But...

what if I wanted it anyway
what if I knew I deserved more
what if I knew I could earn more
and what if I knew that I had unlimited potential

Then one day...

I knew I was worthy
and asked to be paid my value
I knew I could earn more

and I went out and broke that ceiling
I knew that money didn't make people evil
Greed makes people evil
I knew that I deserved every ounce of what I earned
and then I went out and earned some more

Money is a mindset
Prosperity is inherent
Abundance is deserved
There is no shame
We are all worthy of wealth

They were right...

Money doesn't grow on trees
It grows on our beliefs

"Prosperity" by Becca Powers

10 / THE INTERCONNECTEDNESS OF NET WORTH AND SELF-WORTH

"Owning the value you offer the world creates a
powerful ripple effect around you."
—*Marie Forleo*[18]

PART 2 RECAP

Before we begin Part 3, I want to bring you back to look at passion and finding your fire again. During the course of the previous five chapters, we walked through how to awaken to unlimited possibility and we reviewed the top influencers in your life and the roles they play. We talked about the space in-between—where you were and where you are yet to be—and what to expect. Then we talked about empowerment and breaking the limitations that you put on yourself and other people put on you. We went into

---

18 Marie Forleo, "Value What You Do: A Must Watch for Artists & Creatives," Forleo, accessed February 21, 2021, https://www.marieforleo.com/2013/09/value-what-you-do/.

the benefits of opening up to the power of AND—and then breaking old stubborn beliefs and creating new beliefs that support where you are going.

Let's review the five-step process to embracing your passion:

- Step Five: Finding Your Fire

- Step Six: Your Personal Performance Reviews

- Step Seven: The Bridge of In-Between

- Step Eight: The Power of AND

- Step Nine: Set Boundaries, Break Old Patterns, and Create New Policies

PART 3 OVERVIEW

Now that you have reviewed the steps for embracing your passion, Part 3 will focus on providing you steps to help you access your abundance and rise into the role of CEO of your life. We will build your enterprise on the new foundation of healthy self-worth that you worked so hard to restore. Our goal is to have you thrive in your role as CEO. This section is about prosperity, surrounding yourself with supportive relationships, and believing you deserve the very best that life has to offer. It's about living in the expression of joy and ease because you've done the hard work of understanding what you need to thrive. You understand that there is more to life than just surviving.

In the upcoming chapters you will harness your inner CEO. This process is similar to being in a leadership role or having been in your current role at work for several years. You are intimate with the details of what goes on in your day-to-day operations and you are ready for more. You are ready to boss up and protect what makes your world whole. As you do this, you will inspire others with your confidence and conviction. Without trying, you will become a role model just by being authentically you, and others will follow your lead. You will build and maintain a life you love and deserve. And you will have created abundance in more ways than just fiscal.

Chapter 10 has us starting out with embracing your self-worth so you can build your net worth.

BACK TO THE GYPSY THAT I WAS

During my exit interviews at FTP Travel, I had the courage to say things to the executive leadership team—and a few of my peers—that I was afraid to say when I worked there. I was able to articulate that I felt my abilities were held back by their request for me to be Becca lite. I explained that I had a hard time internalizing that into outward action and that, instead, it made me feel limited and small. Although I had nods of acknowledgment, I don't think they had a clue as to just how much damage that one request caused inside me. Secondly, I mentioned how the long 12-hour days away from my home had taken a toll on my family and that the new job would allow me to work from home when I wasn't traveling.

They were curious about this new role and offer. The executive leaders genuinely felt that working at FTP Travel was the best job anyone could ever have. They remained respectful but it was really hard for them to process the idea of people leaving. When I began to share how I was going back to tech to work with Dell again but in a much different role than I had at FTP Travel, they seemed a little perplexed.

I explained that I was going into an outside sales role for large enterprise accounts and that I would be selling technology to executives. I would be in a strategic sales role that was responsible for managing the scope of project transformation goals as a result of taking on new technology during the pre-sales process, ensuring the likelihood of projects closing successfully. Not having a background in tech, they saw this as my taking a self-made demotion.

When I went on to answer their other question, how much I was offered, their faces looked shocked when I replied $175,000. They knew they had recently declined my ask of an additional $10,000, and judging by the wide eyes staring back at me, they realized they had clearly underestimated my value. I told them that I would have been offered a figure in the $200,000s, but because I had taken the decrease in salary to work at FTP, $175,000 was the highest I could get. I shared that within a year I should be able to be back to where I could be in the mid $200,000s as long as I performed well.

I left the office for the last time feeling empowered, with my shoulders back and my head held high. While walking to my car, my energy started to shift. I opened the door to my Durango, sat in the driver's seat, and started the engine, but I had a hard time putting the car into drive. It was like I was frozen. I sat there, staring into the distance, then all of the sudden it was as if I was finally able to authentically emote. What came next was a river of tears. I began ugly crying to the point I couldn't drive. I cried so hard that I could barely see through my tears and my bottom lip was quivering.

What happened in that moment was that I was finally honoring the part of me that had been repressed for all those years, and I was ready to embrace her. If she needed to cry she got to cry. If she needed salt-and-vinegar chips and wine, she got salt-and-vinegar chips and wine. Whatever she needed to do to grieve, I wasn't about to stand her the way.

I ugly cried for about 30 minutes before I was able to drive. I have blonde eyelashes and wear a lot of black mascara, so there were black smears dripping down my face and no napkins in my car. I did my best to use my hands to wipe the smears off; I didn't want to look like a crazy person but I wasn't very successful: the smears remained. I also knew that any minute, my flaming curly red hair was going to get super frizzy. It's something weird that happens when I get upset. So I put on my biggest pair of diva sunglasses to go with my frizzy curls, put on some Fleetwood Mac, and embraced my messy state as I drove myself home.

When I think about that moment now, and how I must have looked to anyone who saw me, it makes me belly laugh. With black tear marks streaming out from underneath oversized tortoise shell sunglasses, rolled down windows blowing my frizzy red curls around—like something between a lion's mane and Bozo the Clown—and Fleetwood Mac's "Gypsy" blaring full blast with me singing along at the top of my lungs, I drove away.

Freeing yourself from a traumatic experience is a little comical in one way and completely liberating in another. As I look back, I recall a lyric from that song "Gypsy" that made me feel like I was returning home to myself. That final drive home from FTP Travel, the Universe gave me a breadcrumb—I was back to being the Gypsy that I was.[19]

ESTABLISHING A NET WORTH

I was already a month or so into the new job and was loving it. My former Dell colleagues welcomed me back with open arms. I was no longer in middle management, I was an outside sales executive selling to some of the largest accounts in South Florida. Lucky for me, my territory included the Florida Keys, which meant I had to head down there at least once a month.

I couldn't believe this was now my life. In this new life, I was able to express myself fully in my role at work. I was able to get paid to drive to the Keys once a month and meet some of the phenomenal people who have chosen island life. They run their businesses well, but there's a little more room to have personal conversations. I was able to befriend a few of my clients who I still stay in touch with to this day.

The drive leaving Miami and taking the two-lane road to the upper Keys is one of the most visually pleasant experiences I have ever had. I had water on both sides of me as far as the eye could see, and a vista filled with light blues, turquoises, and splashes of gold where the sandbars touch the top of the water ever so slightly. On a good day, you can see dolphins jump-

---

19 Fleetwood Mac, "Gypsy," written by Stevie Nicks for *Mirage*, 1982.

ing in the distance. It looks like something out of a travel magazine. Key West is about a four-hour drive from my house, and I love long distance driving by myself. Windows down, music loud, nothing but the wind, my thoughts, and some tunes to create the perfect environment to reconnect with my soul.

On one of my drives to the Keys, I started contemplating my sense of self-worth. I was curious as to where it had gone. Why did it abandon me? Or did I abandon it?

Questions about my self-worth and value continued to run through my head. It was going to take a significant financial recovery to make up for the damage caused by FTP Travel. I had put myself into $40,000 worth of debt to offset the reduced pay I accepted. In addition, I let them get away with never giving me a raise.

It became very apparent to me that there was a direct correlation between my self-worth and my net-worth. I never realized before that there was such a distinct connection between the two. I was starting to feel overwhelmed by the mess that I needed to clean up.

Then, out of nowhere, I remembered that in my new role I was an independent contributor. Being in an independent contributor role is similar to being an entrepreneur but you work for a company. The majority of your income is commission based, with no cap to the amount of commission you could make. Normally, you would start off with few to no sales bookings and very little if any sales pipeline. You develop everything from scratch: I found that thought very refreshing.

For some, sales and entrepreneurship is downright terrifying. Most, if not all, of your income is tied directly to your ability to attract clients, truly offer them a service that converts to a sale, and do it enough that you can survive on your own abilities to create a thriving business. For me, the freedom that comes from having unlimited income potential, becoming a trusted advisor to my clients, and feeling like I'm making an impact in their lives and my family's life makes me feel alive. I feel like I'm making a greater contribution to humanity in some way.

As I drove and reflected on all of this, a sudden curiosity struck me. How much is a human life worth? In my life in corporate America, I have selected my life insurance benefit on more than one occasion. Typically, I see the options range from 100,000 to 250,000 before you really have to come out of your pocket for more coverage. As I contemplated the statistical value of a human life through the eyes of policies, I thought to myself that an average human life is probably worth about $300,000 alive and $3,000,000 dead.

With $300,000 in my mind for my "alive" value, I was beginning to feel empowered that I was beginning to create a healthy value for my net worth. I realized I had some gaps between my self-worth and my net worth, but I could tell they were closing. My offer for my new role was $175,000 *if* I hit my sales quota—it was a big "if." On one side of the coin you can fail miserably and on the other side you have unlimited earning potential.

I started fantasizing about paying off my debt and exceeding my "on target earnings." It seemed pretty fair in my mind that if I was worth $300,000, then I certainly had room to grow into that. My lowest earnings year at FTP Travel was $101,000 and it was apparent that there was a gap in my worth. At that moment, I decided that 2017 was going to be my year of restoration and abundance!

> *Life Hack: If your net worth is low you may want to evaluate your self-worth.*

HELMET CHECK
Decision Breakdown

As I write this book it's toward the end of 2020 and we, all of us in the world, are experiencing our second wave of COVID-19. Facing the grimness of this pandemic and unforeseen death tolls, it's been apparent that the question of life's value has been contemplated by others. A recent article in the *New York Times*, stated that the average American values their life at between $100,000 and $200,000 while alive. Meanwhile, the Consumer Product Safety Commission values a human life at $8.7M alive or dead.[20] When talking about this with my friends and colleagues, almost every single one of them could see their life—at minimum—in the low-end millions when dead. Alive, however, that number was significantly lower, maybe ranging from $100,000 to $500,000. Why the gap? Are we as a society suffering from low self-worth and low self-value?

I'm glad my epiphany back in early 2017 allowed me to own my self-worth and my net worth in a much different way than I had earlier. During these difficult times of COVID-19, it gives me perspective to help others increase their belief in their worth. It's scary to think about leaving debt behind for your loved ones if anything were to happen, or to work all your life and never create the abundance you deserve. If you have yet to ponder the relationship between your self-worth and your net worth, you will get the opportunity in the upcoming exercise, and you'll see where you value yourself today vs where you could be valuing yourself. From there you can work on closing the gap.

---

20   Austin Frakt, "Putting a Value Dollar on Life? Governments Already Do," *New York Times*, May 11, 2020, https://www.nytimes.com/2020/05/11/upshot/virus-price-human-life.html.

MY BELIEFS AROUND RELATIONSHIPS NEEDED A REBOOT

I felt inspired by revisiting my belief systems around self-worth and net worth as it relates to money. Because I had recently identified my old stubborn pattern of needing to be validated and approved of for me to feel worthy, I figured it might be worth exploring my belief system around my relationships, and especially how relationship beliefs impact my self-worth and net worth. I wanted to break free from my self-sabotaging cycles of lowering my worth to be accepted by others.

The truth as I know it, is that our beliefs around our relationships are formed in our childhood. They're formed from our secure relationships, our dysfunctional ones, and our abusive ones. We learned how we need to act to be safe, to feel secure and loved, and to tolerate the intolerable. Our nervous system created the perfect responses for our survival. In one way, we need to thank ourselves for getting us through our childhoods. In another way, we need to create a new way of being because we are no longer children living in our caregivers' environments. Our patterns are outdated and in need of a reboot if we are to move from just surviving to totally thriving.

With that mindset pushing my curiosity, I really needed to get honest with myself to get answers. I knew that at the core of my relationship issues was the belief, "I'm not worthy." I got my pen and paper out, preparing to journal as I asked myself a question: "What does not being worthy look like for me in my relationships?"

Here are some of the answers from that journal entry back in 2017:

- It looks like me being afraid to express what I'm really thinking and feeling.

- It looks like me always pretending to be happy when I'm not.

- It looks like me trying to make broken relationships work because I don't value myself enough to cut them off.

- It looks like me trying to make everyone else happy to prove that I care about them more than myself, as if I'm going to get some type of award for that.

- It looks like me not reaching my potential to keep others comfortable.

It was true, I had outdated programs running the show that would indeed cause my system to crash again if I did not address them.

HEALTHY, HAPPY, AND LOVING RELATIONSHIPS

I was rising into the role of CEO of my life and this was an area where accountability and clean up needed my attention. With two anxiety disorders, adult ADHD, autoimmune disease, and my hair falling out in clumps, I really didn't need much more evidence that my relationship beliefs were in need of a reboot.

As I shared earlier, I had already begun the process of evaluating the people in my life. This part of the process, however, was a little different for me. This was more about how I approached my relationships from a perspective of lowered self-worth. I needed to break the cycle. The future version of me was begging the present me to let her emerge more boldly, more beautifully, and more badass. In order to do so, I needed some new rules and a new foundation to build on.

One day, after returning from one of my work trips to the Keys, I had a spark of inspiration as I was getting ready to take a shower. I remember grabbing my purple dry-erase marker and writing on the mirror in my bathroom:

I am experiencing happy, healthy, and loving relationships that support me from the inside out.

Side Note: Yes, I keep a purple dry-erase marker in my bathroom. Showers are a very sacred part of my daily ritual, probably because of the element of water, which has a key characteristic of renewal. I will often get surges of inspiration either before or after my showers. I need to keep something nearby to write down anything profound that crosses my mind. The dry erase marker does the trick. I have had affirmations written on my bathroom mirrors for well over a decade!

This new affirmation offered a profound new look into my self-worth and net worth, one that I had not yet considered. It was the foundation I needed to build my new beliefs on from the inside out. This meant that I was willing to start with me. What a breakthrough! My life had always been the opposite—the outside dictated how I would feel on my inside. But in writing this one sentence I had just shifted my perspective to be supported from the inside out.

The rest of the affirmation was great too, especially since my relationships typically drained me and took advantage of me. The thought of having healthy, happy, and loving relationships felt incredible—somewhat far-fetched—but incredible. It was the profoundness of recognizing that I was ready to honor my worth and value by living inside out, though, that really propelled me forward in harnessing my inner CEO.

DID YOU GET THE TICKETS?

I have always felt very supported in my relationship with my husband. Jermey and I met back in 2009, when I was working in technology sales and also had my own business as a motivational speaker and coach. I had been single for two years and online dating wasn't going well, but then one day, by a strange twist of luck, our paths crossed.

One of my girlfriends accidentally sent the Fleetwood Mac tickets that she and I had bought to my dating site email address. To this day I don't know how she even had that email address. She texted me saying, "Did you get the tickets?" When I replied, "No." She said, "Check your Yahoo account." Just the thought of logging into my Yahoo account nearly made me barf because I knew I would see the messages from random men from the dating sites I had purposely been avoiding.

As I went to grab the tickets, I saw an email preview from a gentleman who actually wrote, "Dear Rebecca, nice to meet you." There was more to that email, but the fact that he didn't start with "hey baby," "hey sexy," or some other piece of meat calling, and he had a profile picture that showed him with his kids, which clued me in to their priority in his life—were both plusses. I decided to read the email and I found out that he, too, was two years divorced and that his two kids were the same age as mine.

The fact that his email was right above my Fleetwood Mac tickets seemed like a breadcrumb I needed to follow. Fleetwood Mac was my mom's favorite band, and even though she's gone, I still communicate with her through our shared love of music. I took it as a sign and emailed him back.

Jermey and I talked for several weeks, sometimes for hours a day before we met, so I actually knew him when we finally met in person on Saint Patrick's Day 2009. I noticed immediately that we both had Dodge Durangos. We were the same age (59 days apart), we got divorced the same year, our kids were the same age, and we drove the same cars.

We fell in love almost immediately and started blending our family. I have the honor of saying, I'm the proud mom to four wonderful children. At the time of writing this book my daughter, Tyler, is 19, his son, Clayton, is 18. My son, Braydon, is 17, and his daughter, Hailey, is 16. We are the newer version of the Brady bunch.

At the beginning of 2017, our blended family was on edge. My three years at FTP Travel really did a number on all of us. We had spent many of those nights in anger and frustration; patience was thin with each other. To an extent it's not abnormal for a blended family with four teenagers to have a little edge to it. Regardless, I was super aware that our connection as a family unit had paid a price by just trying to power through the circumstances from FTP Travel.

RELATION-SHIFTS AND ACCOUNTABILITY

I'm still unpacking this one, so I don't claim to have my black belt in healthy relationships. I do, however, claim to have made some significant progress that I want to share with you. I found that as my concepts and beliefs around my net worth and self-worth became healthier, there were individuals who would challenge me, saying that I was dreaming too much again. I was increasingly agitated that I was still oversharing and expecting people to support me. I needed to stop that. I also thought that I might have to do another round of performance reviews. But to my surprise, relation-shifts were already happening with little effort from me. And there were those other relationships—like the ones with my spouse and my kids—that acquired effort to amend and repair.

During the time that we were powering through things, what really happened was that nothing was dealt with or acknowledged for years. Words were said that couldn't be taken back, actions had been taken that couldn't be taken back, and lack of action to get things back on track had left its mark on our family. It has taken effort from everyone to get our family back on track—from taking accountability for individual actions that lead to disconnection to forgiveness toward actions that caused us hurt. We are still in the process of healing, but accountability has been a huge factor in our progress.

Even though we have experienced times of being less close as a family unit, we do have moments when we unite as a nucleus of six and it is wonderful. All four of our kids are teenagers now and are coming into their own. They are definitely expressing their individuality—which is exactly what they should be doing.

I do have full confidence that we all will find our way back to each other and live an expression of happy, healthy, and loving relationships within our blended family nucleus. I continue to hold this vision for our family, and I'm astonished to see how the relationships are constantly healing and shifting. No one in our family has to hold back who they are in order to please someone else. Because we allowed everyone to move at their own pace—rather than pushing—it's been a slow process. But because we admitted that things got fucked, invited possibility in with the help of the Universe, and took accountability over our actions, our family unit is more in alignment with that vision now than when I wrote about it in 2017.

I have learned that embracing my self-worth *and* my net worth has helped my children and my husband become more authentically themselves while helping me become more authentically myself. Another thing I learned is that once we are rooted in our new, healthy self-worth, we need to manage our expectations for the results of reprogramming our beliefs. Some areas of life have an immediate shift while others—in my case a large family—have slower shifts. In the end, the relation-shifts do happen and they are healthier, happier, and more loving. When your relationships are supporting you from the inside out, it allows you to honor your self-worth and value your net worth. You find that compromising causes collapsing whereas collaboration creates connection.

PUTTING IT INTO PRACTICE
Step 10: The InterConnectedness of Net Worth and Self-Worth

. . . .

Our relationships, whether with family, friends, or coworkers, are hard things to disentangle. Especially as we embrace our self-worth and build our net worth, others might not feel comfortable with our rise. As we become the CEO of our life, we need our relationships to be supportive.

Up to this point in the book, we have spent most of the time identifying who and what the problems are that derail you from living your truth. You should have a pretty good handle on why certain patterns and behaviors keep boomeranging back into your life, by not exploring how this belief is expressed in your relationships leaves you at risk of not being able to rise into the role of CEO. You won't be able to make decisions based upon what is good for you and your enterprise, only on how others think and feel about what you're doing. And that would mean someone else is the CEO of your life—not you.

With that being said, let's explore how that root belief shows up in the inner working of your relationships, and give this belief a reboot.

There are four parts to the process:

1. Identify your root belief from Chapter 9.

    *   Example: I'm not worthy

2. Write a question to self: What does this belief of ___fill in the blank___ look like for me in my relationships?

    *   Example: What does not being worthy look like for me in my relationships?

3. Answer question to self: *It looks like…* ___finish the sentence___

    *   Example: It looks like I am not reaching my potential in order to keep others comfortable.

4. Create your rebooted affirmation:

    *   Example: I am experiencing happy, healthy, and loving relationships that support me from the inside out.

Fill out the following with your own information and reference the above for guidance.

1. Identify your root belief from Chapter 9:

   _____

2. Write a question to self: What does this belief of __fill in the blank__ look like for me in my relationships?

   _____

   _____

3. Answer question to self: *It looks like*... __finish the sentence__ (up to 3 answers)

   It looks like: _____

   It looks like: _____

   It looks like: _____

4. Create your rebooted affirmation:

   _____

   _____

What are you more aware of now that you have completed the exercise?

_____

_____

Write about a time from your past when compromising your needs for someone else's led to a collapse.

_____

_____

Write about a time from your past when collaboration with someone else led to deeper connection.

_____

_____

EXERCISE
Closing the Net Worth Gap
. . . .

Now that you have your self-worth in check, it's time to take a look at your net worth. We will look at what value you put on a living human being and where you fall on that spectrum. If there is a gap, we will enter into the realm of unlimited possibility to visualize you are closing it, and with the hope that it inspires you to close the gap in your real life. Finances are an area that a lot of people like to turn their head away from. If you are one of those people, I promise you will make it through the exercise just fine. To really harness your inner CEO, you need to earn your value. Typically, I see my clients overworked and underpaid. This exercise will help you take a look at that. We will start by identifying how you value a live human life.

What value do you put on a human life?

_____

_____

What value do you put on your life right now?

_____

_____

What is the gap between how you value someone else's life and your own?

_____

_____

Now, you might be saying, "I'll never get that gap closed," and I would say, "That's limited thinking, and we should explore other possibilities." Right now the gap might not close overnight, but if you keep actioning in the direction of your worth—step-by-step, day-by-day, week-by-week— you will see your net worth increase.

Let's open the door to possibility and explore some questions that could provide a path for you to increase your net worth.

In your profession, what are the ranges of pay, where do you fall on the scale, and why?

_____

_____

What are your creative passions, and what could you charge for others to enjoy them?

_____

_____

What services are you giving away to others, and could you charge for them?

_____

_____

What dreams do you have that have gone unfulfilled? Is it possible to make money following your dreams? If so, what are the income possibilities?

_____

_____

If you have or could have a side hustle what would it be? How much is the income potential?

_____

_____

What did you find most insightful about this exercise?

_____

_____

Over time, you will find that as you embrace your self-worth, opportunities appear for you to build your net worth. As you get more comfortable with this concept, you will find it easier to say yes to new opportunities that previously you may have turned down. Possibility awaits.

You can return to the exercise anytime at: https://www.beccapowers.com/worksheetshyic

SHERRI

Sherri and I met at work. She was 17 and I was freshly 18. Having turned 18 on the 13th of December, I was just a few weeks into my adulthood when I started working at Concept Stores. I didn't know it then, but this job would be the start of my sales career.

I hadn't been there for more than a couple days when Sherri handed me the keys to the store and said she was leaving early. She had met a guy at a New Year's Eve party and had a chance to see him again. If I could hold down everything at the store she would be able to go. I told her to go and have fun!

We still laugh about how we first met. Something about the way that went down made us instant friends. Here we are 20-plus years later and still best friends. When I think about someone who embraced their self-worth to build their net worth, I think of Sherri.

Sherri and her two brothers were raised by her beautiful mom, Julie. As a single mom, Julie often had to work two or three jobs just to keep a roof over their heads and food on the table. There were times when food was rationed and when they went without to make ends meet. The one thing they never went without was love, but for a teenager, that can only take you so far. Sherri started working as soon as she could.

Sherri and I both started our careers in retail. Both of us were recognized early on for our drive and capability. We both spent the start of our 20s in retail management. I ended up not liking management as much as I liked sales. Sherri ended up not liking sales as much as she enjoyed management and the operations aspect of the role.

As time went on and we approached our mid-20s, Sherri started reflecting on the direction her life was going. She was an assistant manager for Sprint PCS. On the surface, that seemed pretty good for someone her age. But as she started to look toward the future, she knew would be limiting herself if she continued down that path.

Her mom had remarried and recently moved from our hometown of Coral Springs, Florida, relocating to a town outside Atlanta, Georgia. As Sherri contemplated what to do next with her life, going to college and getting a degree while she was still young enough was at the top of the list. I still remember how shocked and in awe of her I was when she told me what she was considering.

Sherri said to me, "Bec, I've been thinking about moving back in with my mom to get my degree. I'm thinking of getting an engineering degree. I would start off at a junior college and if I do well enough, I'll transfer to Georgia Tech."

I said, "That sounds like a fantastic idea!"

Sherri worked on the arrangements and within a couple months was off to Georgia. Life was tough for a bit. She moved back in with her mom after seven years or so of living on her own, and she stopped working. After making close to $50,000 a year, it was hard not to earn a paycheck, but Sherri persevered in the most incredible way despite the hardships. She knew she was worth it and stayed committed to the vision even during the hard times.

Sherri did end up graduating from Georgia Tech at the top of her class. She received her degree in Industrial Engineering. She began working as an engineering consultant immediately following her graduation. As a result, she doubled what she was making in retail! Talk about that self-worth and net worth gap closing. She straight out redefined her worth, value, and what she was capable of!

Today, Sherri is happily married with a son. With the relocation to Georgia years ago, she is surrounded by her family and enjoys raising her son immersed in happy family time.

11 / EXECUTIVE DREAM TEAM

> *"A mentor is someone who allows you*
> *to see the hope inside yourself."*
> —Oprah Winfrey[21]

A SALES TALE OF EPIC PROPORTION

I remember standing in front of a room presenting to about 20 Dell sellers—specifically, the Dell EMC storage team. I had only been back in the swing of things for six months or so and was already closing a ton of business. On this particular day, I was presenting the deals I had recently closed, the use cases behind them, and the pipeline I'd created. I was so excited to show off all my hard work, and I was hopeful that more of the sellers would give me an opportunity to work with them after they'd seen what I could do.

---

21 "Oprah Winfrey: Who Mentored Oprah Winfrey," Harvard School of Public Health, accessed February 21, 2021, https://sites.sph.harvard.edu/wmy/celebrities/oprah-winfrey/.

I was at the front of the room with the audience facing me from a U-shaped table. I had my presentation clicker in hand and all eyes were on me. The room was fully engaged in the customer story I was telling, one of the most epic tales I have experienced in my career.

The story starts with Jermey and I packing up the car at 6:30 in the morning to head down to the Keys for another week of customer visits. I had to be in Key West for a couple of days so I decided to extend the invitation to my husband and see if we could ask the grandparents to watch the kids. They said "yes" and I finally got to bring Jermey down to Key West and show him everything I'd been doing. I was looking forward to taking him out to some of the restaurants that I've really enjoyed, introducing him to some of my clients, and giving him an opportunity to relax poolside while I went to work.

We hit the road early in a bid to miss South Florida rush hour. I had my first appointment at lunchtime so this gave us enough time to get down to Key West, check into the hotel, and get me to my client on time. We were about 30 minutes into the drive when I got an email followed by a phone call from one of the Directors of IT that I was working with. One of their trays in their storage array had stopped working and brought down their systems. This was a level 10 emergency for the client.

I had to pull over, change seats with my husband to let him drive, pull out both my cell phones and my laptop, activate one cell phone as a hotspot to connect to my laptop and then use my other phone to start making calls. Talk about work in action.

My client needed a storage array ASAP. I immediately called my engineer Shawn who was already en route on the ferry to Key West. There was another engineer who was meeting us down there named Keith. Shawn suggested that I call Keith to see if he might have an extra storage array in his garage that he could bring down. Keith lives in Jupiter which is about a four-hour drive to Key West. I was super nervous that he had already hit the road.

I called Keith twice and no answer. I was freaking out because the client was in an absolutely horrible situation. Ordering a new storage array was completely possible but would take a minimum of two to four weeks to get there. We had to get their environment back up to full operational in a couple hours. As full-blown panic began to set in, Keith called me back.

"Are you still home?" I asked.

"Yes," he said. "I was loading up the car and saying goodbye to the family when you called. What's up?"

I explained the situation and its urgency, and then said, "Please tell me you have something in your garage you can bring down with you."

Keith replied, "Actually, I do!"

We were ready to rock. I called the Director of IT and told her that we had a spare that we would bring down with us and I would work on getting an order together for a new one. She was light-staffed and needed engineering support to help trade the units out. I had not planned for a customer emergency and had several client meetings scheduled. I kept my cool with my customer, but inside I was beginning to panic again at the thought of needing to cancel my other meetings.

I called Shawn back and let him know that Keith was coming to the rescue with a spare and would be in Key West around 11. I asked Shawn what we should do about the meetings and he said that he would handle the install and to take Keith to the meetings. I was like, *phew!* This whole process of coordinating and making sure that everything was going to work out took a solid two hours.

Jermey and I arrived at the hotel, checked in and got the luggage to the room. I decided to have him drive me to the customer site to meet Keith so I could ride with him to our meetings and leave Jermey my Durango. Upon arrival, my firefighter/hero husband offered to carry this heavy ass storage array into the client site. I introduced Jermey to my client. She was so relieved that we were there with a solution to her problem that I saw her eyes start to tear up.

Shawn's ferry was a little delayed and it didn't look like he would be there until noon. Jermey decided to head back to the hotel and Keith and I left for our first meeting. After Shawn arrived at our client site to switch out the units, I got a call from him saying he really needed some help, just an extra set of hands to move some of the gear around, turn screwdrivers, stuff like that. I really needed Keith to stay with me for the more technical aspects of our meetings so I quickly asked, "Are you cool if I send my husband?"

Shawn responded, "If he's willing, absolutely."

I called Jermey and asked him, "Honey, would you mind going back to the client site? Shawn needs a helping hand." Jermey being a hero by nature said, "Yeah babe, whatever you need."

He got back in the Durango and headed over to meet Shawn. Another crisis averted!

WHEN THINGS ARE GOOD, GREAT CAN BE AROUND THE CORNER

I finished the story and everyone in the audience was cheering and clapping—some even stood up as they celebrated my victory. I was beaming ear to ear in pride. A sales tale of this epic proportion does not happen often and I was thrilled that I could tell such a story. Then something happened that totally shifted my energy—a Gmail notification popped up on my laptop screen and the subject line read: Riverbed Technologies would like to interview you!

My heart dropped to my stomach and I cleared the notification as fast as possible. Luckily, no one saw it but me. It took me a moment to regain my composure. I had left my personal email open during my PowerPoint presentation, not thinking that I would be getting any emails like that!

I had forgotten that I had given Jessica my résumé a month earlier. Jessica was now at Riverbed Technologies, and she had given my résumé to her leader. Apparently, the Universe decided to gift me an interview at the very moment I was trying to build my business and brand with Dell.

The meeting ended on a high note and everyone in the room was now comfortable working with me, they believed I would do right by their customers, and they were willing to trust me. Mission accomplished. Although I left that meeting on a high, as soon as I got back into the Durango, I had to collect myself. The Universe had just sent me a breadcrumb and I knew I needed to follow it. Saying "yes" to exploring opportunities is my agreement with the Universe. I don't have to say "yes" to the overall opportunity but I do need to say "yes" to exploring it.

This left me with an inner conflict. I had successfully built up the trust I needed to take my business to the next level. It was no easy feat to do that, but here in my email in-box was something that might align with me even better. Oh boy, I thought to myself, here we go again!

I did indeed follow the breadcrumbs and everything about Riverbed was perfect, down to my face-to-face interview with my soon-to-be boss who walked in all executive-like with a pair of Beats around his neck, signaling a fellow music lover. I knew that I was going to break $200,000 if I stayed in my current role supporting Dell, so I expressed that I would need a really solid offer to encourage me to leave. Riverbed offered me $240,000 to join their team and excitedly I said, "Yes!" It's a lesson that stays with me today, when things are good, great is waiting around the corner if we only have the courage to look.

Life hack: When things are good, great can be around the corner. Be ready.

TEAM AWESOME IS BACK

I was thrilled to be working with Jessica again. Not only is she my work BFF but she is my earth angel for always seeing my potential and not allowing me to settle. Back in our days at ScriptLogic, we shared territory. In addition to that, she ended up sitting next to me for a bit. After becoming friends and respecting each other professionally, we decided to partner up and market together. We named ourselves Team Awesome. We drove the office crazy with Team Awesome. People hated it—but I think they envied it. By partnering up, we drove up our customer interaction and crushed our sales goals. Team Awesome had been a dynamic duo and now we were back together.

Riverbed Technology felt like a perfect fit from day one. I was familiar with the technology because I'd had the opportunity to sell it back in 2009 when I worked for Modcomp Solutions, a regional technology partner in South Florida. The culture was a wonderful fit—Riverbed was filled with good people who had a strong sense of work hard, play hard. It was understood that you were there to perform and as sellers we knew that our job was at risk if we didn't, so there was no need for micromanaging.

By that point in my career, I had achieved President's Club six times—overachieving my sales goal by more than 100 percent—quite the feat. I was relieved to see how Riverbed respected its talent. That level of respect was something I was deprived of all those years at FTP Travel. Instead of being asked to turn down my volume, I was being asked to turn it up! I felt clear on my expectations and I was ready to kick some ass. For the first time in a long time in my career, I felt seen.

Four weeks into the role, my boss called me and said, "I want to tell you before the company makes the announcement. We are creating a commercial team that you will be aligned with as of next week." That meant my current team would be divided into two—commercials accounts and enterprise accounts. I was being moved to the commercial team, which meant I would focus on accounts that produced one to two billion in revenue. Enterprise would focus on accounts that produced two billion and greater in revenue.

Although I was bummed that I wouldn't be reporting to my director any longer or be on the same team as Jessica, I knew that everything was unfolding exactly as it should. My guard was down and was officially in a dance with the Universe. Everything about the announcement felt good, and I was trusting my intuition that I was being guided again to a better opportunity.

INSTANT CRUSH AND IT'S NOT WHAT YOU THINK

The following week I was transferred to the commercial team. My new team leader, Cortez, was a new hire to Riverbed as well. He was smart, cool, collected, and did an excellent job giving us vision, setting expectations, and building a collaborative team. I eventually ended up calling him "Coach" because I felt like he ran our team like a sports team—which I loved.

In fact, I loved everything about Riverbed, from its people to its product and to its culture. I really didn't think my work life could get any better. Within the first month or so of being on the commercial team we all received an invitation for a sales and segment kick-off in San Francisco. Our senior leadership wanted us to rally up and get excited about the opportunity ahead of us. They wanted to prove to us that creating a commercial segment was the right choice and get us fired up to crush it.

A few weeks later, the morning after the flight to San Francisco, I showed up at our corporate offices bright and early in order to get a seat up front. The corporate trainers opened the session with what to expect, rules of the day—that type of thing.

Following the opening, they introduced our VP of sales, and Jillian Man-solf walked on stage—a beautiful executive woman, standing in her power, delivering a message with clarity, confidence, and data. She had hired inde-pendent companies, leveraged our internal analytical teams, and presented the data back to us in a bite-size digestible format. She had studied all the data in our segment to understand buying patterns, wallet-share opportu-nities, segmentations that align specifically to our business, as well as the annual revenue trends for the past several years. My jaw dropped.

On top of that, Jillian Mansolf was absolutely stunning. Tall, fit, with long black hair, she oozed a rock 'n' roll edge and a "don't fuck with me" at-titude. She was a master strategist. I'm pretty sure I had an instant mentor crush within the first two minutes.

As a skilled strategist myself, I had to meet her! I knew that I wanted to mentor under her. She was just so rad. To see a woman up there in her power and in her element like that, it was so empowering!

Now, although I definitely have a touch of "I am woman, hear me roar" in me, I want to make sure I highlight that I absolutely appreciate men and in no way mean to negate them. Men have an incredible ability to offer simplicity to counterbalance our complexity and to have conviction when we are still confused or pondering. If you have a chance to mentor under a man you trust, I would focus on the two gifts they inherently pos-sess: simplicity and conviction. Jillian Mansolf had both of those gifts, so I knew that somewhere along the way she had been mentored by the best. I wanted in.

After the presentation, Jillian stuck around for questions and multiple people approached her. I stood to the side and waited my turn. I didn't want to be rushed and I didn't want to have a bunch of people standing around us, so I waited until the throng subsided before I approached her. In typical Becca fashion, I boldly said, "What you did up there was rad. I can tell you're a brilliant strategist and I want in. I already have a major girl crush on you and I don't know what to do about it." I laughed as I finished up my opening line. She greeted me back with a huge smile and laughed. She said, "I don't know that I've ever been approached like that before but I'm flattered." She told me she didn't have much time left to talk but said I could sit with her at dinner and we could have a deeper conversation. I was thrilled!

DINNER WITH THE GODDESS OF STRATEGY

I used the happy hour to mingle and get to know my coworkers better since I was new at the company. I knew that at dinner I would get to spend time with Jillian—who I had already nicknamed the Goddess of Strategy—and I could ask her all the questions I wanted.

I synced up with Jillian and sat down for dinner. I didn't want to start sweating, so I took my jacket off from over my dress tank top and put it on the back of the chair. Jillian leaned over and said, "killer tats, do you play music?" She was referring to the tattoos I have on my shoulder blades. I have dedicated the left shoulder blade to my mom with piano keys and flowers and my right shoulder blade to my dad with a guitar and flowers. I answered, "No, but my parents do," without getting into the details of their passing.

I told her how my parents were full-time musicians when I was born, and that I grew up around live music and still love going to concerts more than just about anything. She saw my wedding ring and asked, "Is your husband a musician too?" I responded, "No, he is a firefighter/paramedic but my ex-husband was." She laughed and said, "The opposite for me. My ex-husband didn't play anything but my boyfriend is a musician for a touring band."

We had a great rapport going and ended up continuing our conversation on music. She asked me what one of my favorite bands was and I said, "Fleetwood Mac."

"Awesome," she responded. "I love a lyric from one of their songs that goes: *lightning strikes maybe once, maybe twice.*"

"I know exactly what song that is, that's 'Gypsy'," I said. I paused for a moment. Before I continued, I had a flashback to my final drive home from FTP Travel when I had "Gypsy" blaring from the stereo. I knew the Universe had just given me a breadcrumb. I continued where I left off and asked Jillian, "Why does that line mean something to you?"

Jillian replied, "I am dating my high school sweetheart again after 20 years and it's absolutely magical. I feel like that lyric. Lightning strikes maybe once, maybe twice, and I'm very aware I'm on my second strike." Just when I thought I couldn't be more in awe of this strategy goddess she goes and says something like that.

She eventually asked me a little about my career, especially my background related to strategy. She recognized that I noticed something specific in her. We started chatting about our backgrounds and chuckled when we realized we were both formerly at Dell.

She was much higher up in the company than I was and worked for them much earlier in her executive career. She was at the company and reported very closely to Michael Dell before the company had mastered the art of customer segmentation. Customer segmentation is huge, especially once there is an existing sales funnel, because it provides a more specialized customer service experience that improves customer retention and therefore allows the sales people to focus their efforts on creating more opportunities.

Dell changed the way large organizations think about their go-to market approach and Jillian was part of that revolutionary change. I shared with her how, as a sales leader, strategy had always been my strength as well. I shared that I had, in fact, changed the way two of the organizations I worked for presented customer data to the salespeople, which had a significant impact on increased revenue.

I, too, had had my own revolutionary experiences, and I could see that what I was saying resonated with Jillian. I could see her reflect not only approval but awe. We were speaking the same language and she could see me, the real me, the Becca who is extremely talented, expansive, and a goddess in her own right.

Something happened that night: another round of the Grinch Effect occurred, but instead of my heart growing three times, it was my confidence. It was then that I realized the power of a mentor. I saw something in Jillian that I loved about myself. She, in turn, reflected back that she saw it in me too.

I was just being authentically me. I was owning my worth. I was sharing my passion for music and business unfiltered. In return, I received in one evening what I had been looking for since the day my initial wound reopened back in 2014. There, in a restaurant in San Francisco in early 2018, I reunited with my awesomeness and was able to own my talents and gifts unapologetically.

TIME FOR AN EXECUTIVE DREAM TEAM

I left that dinner feeling confident and empowered. As I was walking through the streets of San Francisco back to my hotel, a thought floated across my mind like a whisper. I heard the words from my former VP of sales, Markeith, "You are CEO of your own life."

My heart began to race with excitement. I thought to myself, if I am CEO of my own life, then my life must be the enterprise. That led to the next thought: there isn't a thriving enterprise I know of that doesn't have an advisory board of executives sitting at the helm. These executives have experience in specific aspects of the business where they offer their expertise and provide critical insight as well as checks and balances to ensure the overall health and growth of the organization.

That was it! I wanted to build an executive dream team of my own. But how would I structure it? As I pondered that for a minute, I broke it down into three categories: mentor, coach, public figure. I really liked where my thought pattern was going, and I knew that I wanted to create an executive dream team.

I grabbed a pen and paper and wrote down a short list of some of the mentors, coaches, and public figures I knew I wanted on my dream team. Here's what I wrote:

- Strategy and Sales Career: Jillian Mansolf, mentor

- Public Speaking and Entrepreneurship: AmondaRose Igoe, coach-turned-mentor

- Kundalini Yoga: Master teacher Deva Kaur, teacher and mentor

- Spirituality and Universal Law: Gabby Bernstein, spiritual teacher; Gina Lorenzo, one of Gabby's spirit junkie coaches

Note: This list has continued to evolve as I evolve.

PUTTING IT INTO PRACTICE:
Step 11: Your Executive Dream Team
. . . .

Before we build your executive dream team, we are going to define the role of each member type so you can identify them properly. Your Executive Dream Team (EDT) is a cast of different characters from the ones we identified earlier—partner, family, friends, and fan club—who provide you healthy support. We worked on those elements in previous chapters.

The individuals on your EDT are masters of their craft. They should embody the very thing you are looking to achieve. For example, although you might love your mom, if you were to ask her how to become a *New York Times* best-selling author, you would probably never become one because she lacks that experience. However, if you were to hire an author who is also a coach who has a *New York Times* best seller under their belt, the likelihood of your becoming one yourself significantly increases.

Let's do a quick review of the different types of members for your Executive Dream Team.

- The Mentor: Someone who emulates success in an area of life that you are focusing on and who you can reach out to, from time to time, for guidance. There are some structured programs through corporate offerings and nonprofits that offer mentorship programs that you can apply for. I have found my mentors either through identifying them as someone I want to learn from and asking them for mentorship, or by hiring them as a coach and staying in touch with them for occasional mentorship. This might be your coach from a sports team, a teacher from one of your classes, or a leader in your organization, for example.

- The Coach: Someone you invest in to give you a system and support toward achieving the outcome you desire. This is typically offered in two styles: private coaching and group coaching. A lot of group programs offer a private group option so you can be among cohorts who are focused on the same subject for additional support and motivation. I have made some amazing friends who have supported the future version of me in this way. They normally offer books, lectures, workshops, and online courses as an alternative means of interacting with them for a lower investment than the coaching programs.

- The Public Figure: Someone who, in the eyes of the public, has become a subject matter expert (SME). These are thought leaders in the area you are looking to focus on. They might be authors, motivational speakers, musicians, or sports coaches, for example, and are visible on multiple social media platforms, including podcasts, vlogs, YouTube. It's possible that you already follow them.

Now that we have some framework around your EDT member types, let's identify some that you have used in the past.

In each category, list up to three that you have worked with in the past.

Mentors:

_____

_____

_____

Coaches:

_____

_____

_____

Public Figures:

_____

_____

_____

After writing down the names of people you've turned to in the past as unofficial members of your executive dream team, what stands out the most about who you have been interacting with and following?

_____

_____

_____

EXERCISE

Build Your Executive Dream Team

· ·

This part is so exciting and inspiring because you are building the very team that can see and support your new vision for yourself. Here we are going to identify five executive members for your dream team.

My clients typically select their dream team based on those who can lend expertise in these four categories:

- Amplify a Natural Strength: An area of natural heightened ability that can be amplified.

- Strengthen an Area of Opportunity: An area of natural challenge that can be improved upon.

- Desire to Learn: A topic that you would like to learn more deeply, with more exposure.

- Necessity to Learn: The need to learn information in response to a life event or circumstance.

Before we get started, I want to break down strengths and weaknesses a little more. For example, I am a visionary: I do extremely well in strategic roles that focus on creating new visions. Whether I'm helping a customer transform their IT infrastructure or I'm working one-on-one with my coaching clients to create a life that aligns with their desires, this is a strength of mine. I have an ability to see the new vision, understand how all the pieces will work together, put a transition plan in place, and create a system for implementation. This is my gift of iterative, strategic thinking. When I surround myself with mentors in this strength, I benefit both from my capacity to learn quickly and my ability to immediately implement the learning.

Now let's talk about over-correcting a weakness. This topic drives me nuts. I see so many people invest so much money into their weaknesses. While, yes, a weakness can be improved upon, it's not always going to improve. It's a weakness for the reason that it's not one of your strengths.

Can you imagine if Beyoncé was hyper-focused on her weakness rather than her strength? Let's say she is terrible at tennis. Every time she played tennis as a kid she lost and was made fun of. In an effort to prove all the haters wrong, she invested in the best tennis coaching available and improved, but only to be a mediocre tennis player at best. With only middle-level improvement, Beyoncé walked around feeling defeated.

Meanwhile, ever since Beyoncé was a toddler, she'd had the ability to sing and perform. It felt so natural and a part of her that she dismissed it, not recognizing that it was a true gift. Instead of developing her craft to become the Beyoncé we all know and love, she focused so much on tennis that she missed her calling. Can you imagine a world without Sasha Fierce?

Luckily for us that's not what happened. Beyoncé knew her strengths and talents and dedicated her life to bringing them forward for the world to enjoy. She said "screw it" to tennis and "hell yes" to singing and performing. Now, I don't know if Beyoncé is a terrible tennis player or not. I just made that up, but it's a good representation of how different things can be if we focus on our weaknesses instead of our strengths.

Now it's your turn to select five executives for your dream team. Remember, you can reference the self-assessments in Chapter 1 and Chapter 7 to help pull forward areas for selection. In this section, you'll see examples of my own executive dream team, followed by a space to create your own. Write down who they are, their corresponding area of specialty, and the personal goal they represent in your life. Here are five as an example from my current list:

Name	Specialty	Personal Goal
Nancy Levin	Master coach and author	Write and publish a book
Mastin Kipp	Trauma coach and author	Write and publish a book
Suzanne Gundersen	Trauma practitioner, EFT	Heal, feel free and happy
Ali Miller, R.D.	Functional nutritionist	Heal with food as medicine
Jennifer Cichoski	Cisco sales director	Maximize Cisco career

	Name	Specialty	Personal Goal
1.	_____		
2.	_____		
3.	_____		
4.	_____		

You can return to the exercise anytime at: https://www.beccapowers.com/worksheetshyic

AMONDAROSE IGOE

AmondaRose is one of my coaches who has turned into a mentor and friend. I started working with her back in 2008 when I first had dreams of being a writer, speaker, and coach. She is an acclaimed public-speaking coach in the South Florida area, with clients all over the world. Her specialty is teaching small business owners and entrepreneurs how to clearly and confidently share their message, heart to heart. When this sort of connection happens, it is easy for her clients to captivate their audience and compel them to move forward with investing in their products and services.

When I first started on this path, I hired her to help me put my signature talks together. I also enlisted her guidance on starting my business: she embodied so many things that I was seeking.

Over the years she has shifted from being my coach to being my mentor. I took a detour back into corporate America and put my writing and speaking on hold; I continued to coach and mentor but on a referral basis and on the side rather than full-time. I mention that because I didn't need as much help building my signature talks and refining my story to connect with people. It was natural for our relationship to switch roles. However, I always kept AmondaRose on my executive dream team.

She has been CEO of her own business for over 15 years and I have continued to attend her events. She is always evolving, constantly stretching herself, up-leveling her programs, building in bonuses, and changing lives and businesses in the process. AmondaRose is the epitome of how to create a life you love on your own terms: she lives on the beach with her husband and two dogs; vacations frequently; and loves what she does for a living. She took herself from making $25,000 a year, to making over six figures, to producing six-figure events that she hosts several times a year. And those things don't take into account all the other aspects of her business that are not associated with her big events. She has a full but simple life that she absolutely enjoys.

I'm proud that I get to call her a friend, a mentor, and a coach. As I was wrapping up writing this book, we had discussions about hiring her as my coach again to assist with my signature talks. This is a prime example of why it's important to have an executive dream team. AmondaRose has been a member of my EDT for over a decade. She's connected to me and my vision. I know without a doubt that I am working with someone who not only has my back, but wants to see me succeed.

If you are in the market to bring your story, your message, and your heart to more people, I recommend that you look her up. She just might inspire your inner CEO the way she has inspired mine: to do what I love, make money doing it, and live the life I dream—because it's possible.

12 / OWNING IT ALL

*"You attract the right things when you
have a sense of who you are."*

—Amy Poehler[22]

LEVEL 2

A few months after returning from San Francisco, I had a kundalini level-two training module scheduled. It was set to start in October 2018. In the level-two certification process in kundalini there are five modules. Each one of them is life changing in its own right. The fastest that you can complete the level-two training is two and half years. Personally, I allow at least a year in between modules to integrate all the shifts that occur during those powerful six-to-eight days of transformation.

One of my soul sisters, Pamela, drove across from Naples so we could take this module together. As we prepared for our next magic carpet ride to the magical kingdom of self-transformation, we were both equally excited

---

22 Amy Poehler's Smart Girls, "Letting Go: Ask Amy," YouTube video, December 6, 2012, https://www.youtube.com/watch?v=4iCHN-PzUlU&feature=youtu.be.

and terrified. No one emerges from a level-two training the same person they were when they went in.

POP

This level-two module was Lifecycles & Lifestyles, which helps you gain perspective on generational trauma and the timeline of your recurring patterns. It provides yogic wisdom about the cycles in life, when they occur, and why. I knew there would be a lot to unpack in this training.

In this specific class, there were about 45 of us: a mix of about 85 percent women and 15 percent men. Many of us knew each other from having taken various training sessions together. That helped to make it more comfortable to reach the level of vulnerability we needed to get to the tender space that creates healing and integrates lasting change. Simply put, these level twos are about healing the healer. That being said, everyone was pretty committed to their healing journey at this point in the process. Level twos are intense.

By the end of the second day we were all in energetic sync. Our chanting was in sync as if we were one voice. Our breathing was in sync as if we were one breath. You could just feel it. We were on the final meditation of the day and were putting everything we had into it. Working our breath and connecting with the mantra, you could feel the energy we were creating cycling through the room. As we neared the end, the chanting and breathing grew super intense. We were one.

Suddenly, there was a big electrical POP! Everyone gasped and then laughed as we realized we had blown out the power: the energy we produced as a group was out of this world. Our master teachers, Deva Kaur and Kirn Khalsa, were impressed with our electrical blowout. When the power came on again, just a few seconds later, they rallied us back together to finish where we had left off and end the class for the day. We left feeling powerful in an expansive kind of way.

The next day was day three and the final day of this weekend of training. Pamela and I arrived, walked in the door, and immediately shared a look of panic. The sultry conditions indoors meant only one thing—the air conditioner was out. It was only 9:45 a.m. and already 90 degrees in the room. October may be autumn in other areas of the US but for us Floridians it is still hot as hell. Apparently that big electrical pop the night before was the A/C, and the repair guy wasn't going to be able to make it until 3:00 p.m.

Our master teachers spared us no mercy; they said the show must go on, reinforcing the concept that life is about dealing with the circumstances that are handed to us. Today we were being given the circumstance of no A/C. Pamela and I were already laughing because we knew this was going to be shit show. Deep down we were both nervous because we also knew it was going to be transformational as hell. We were preparing ourselves for one of our biggest magic carpet rides yet.

We started the morning with a 90-minute kriya and meditation combo. By the end of it, 80 percent of the class was down to sports bras for the ladies and no shirts for the men. Yoga pants were rolled up as far as they could go and those lucky enough to have worn shorts underneath their pants, had the additional relief of taking off their pants.

The crankiness level in the room was starting to turn up along with the heat. I would say about 60 percent of the class was women over 50 and the majority of them were in menopause. It was not a good time to piss off any of the ladies.

Within minutes of finishing the kriya, Deva Kaur's husband, Deva Singh, showed up with half a dozen industrial-sized fans to help cool us down. You would have thought God himself had arrived by the amount of cheering and applause that broke out. The women over 50 fought for first rights to the fans. Pamela and I stayed back; we knew better than to get involved.

I AM THE LIONESS

The fans helped reduce the temperature from 95 degrees down to about 90 degrees. It was still way too hot to think about anything other than being hot. After the break from our morning kriya, we began our first experience of the day. We were guided by Kirn through a meditation of ancestral knowledge. There was strong tribal and ceremonial drumming in the background that became the soundtrack of our transformational experience.

Kirn guided us back in time to meet our ancestral tribe members and went on to explain that we would be coming in contact with aspects of our past that contain some of our deepest wisdom. Kirn's talk track was in perfect alignment with the tribal drum beats. It was the perfect combination to send us back in time to a place where we were one with the land like our Native American and Aboriginal brothers and sisters. I saw myself as myself—but not. I recognized that my soul was me, but my body was different.

I was thin, extremely fit, and in my prime. My skin was perfect: unblemished, dark brown, and burnished by the sun. My hair was cropped so short I was nearly bald. I had turquoise painted stripes under each eye. I had bracelets all the way up to my mid-forearm. Each bracelet meant something. I understood that these bracelets showed my specialties and symbolized my status.

I was revered within my tribe. I was one of the rising matriarchs. I had many responsibilities within my tribe. I was a healer and a hunter. I hunted small creatures mainly for medicinal and ceremonial reasons. I studied under the masters within the tribe, learning everything about how we were one with the land and spirit. I understood that I would eventually be taking the lead as one the key tribe members over ceremony and ritual. This was a big deal and required years of preparation. I remember feeling very proud to have this honor.

I dropped back into this life for a moment. My heart was racing as I recognized the part of that life that is within me in this life. Simultaneously, I have parts of that life that are lying dormant while other parts are awakened. My entire body was drenched in sweat and I sympathized with the menopausal women who were freaking out during our morning kriya.

I wasn't left in this body for long before I was led back to my vision. My soul was longing to return to the tribal experience and join the beating of the drums. When I returned there, I was dancing wildly around the fire. I was encouraging my other tribe members to join in the ceremonial drum circle.

I heard Kirn guide us to invite our animal totem into our experience. Once she offered that suggestion, I saw myself and members of my tribe enacting various animal behaviors as we danced around the fire. The drumbeat was getting faster. My dance moves were getting more erratic. Our breathing in the class was getting stronger. Kirn then asked for us to come face to face with our animal totem. There in my vision, she entered: the Lioness.

Prior to this experience I had never gravitated to lions before. However, this time was different. She was everything I needed to know and embrace. The Lioness doesn't second guess that she's a Lioness. She is confident in her role and knows exactly what to do with it. The Lioness is fierce, independent, loyal, brave, strong, and agile. She is the primary hunter and provider for the pride and is insanely protective of her cubs. I knew her when she showed herself to me as if we had been old friends. I had some choices to make: I could ignore her, I could have her walk with me, or I could merge with her and embody her. I chose to merge with her.

Kirn began to wind down the experience. In doing so she asked us, "What message does your totem have for you? I want you to keep the answer at the top of your mind. You will be writing down this experience as you come out of it." She continued to wrap things up. Once we were still, she said, "Now open your eyes and write down what your totem said to you."

The Lioness said to me, "You look too much for guidance outside your-self. It made you abandon your pride, yourself, and your kids. Embody me. You will question yourself no more and all will be restored." Tears ran down my face, merging with the sweat droplets that were covering my skin. There was a truth in her words that was resonating to the depths of me.

Kirn then said, "Write down your animal totem, then you have 10 min-utes to free write from this experience. The volunteers will walk around the room to pass out popsicle sticks. On these sticks you will write the message from your totem. Write it in such a way that you will always remember it."

Here I was, dripping in sweat and tears, feeling like I'd just taken a bunch of magic mushrooms. My mind was somewhere between the cosmos and this classroom. I was trying my best to reel myself back into my body. I was perplexed as to how to take something of this magnitude and bring it down to a single sentence, a sentence that would serve as my guide if I get too far off my path.

I was finally given my popsicle stick. In reaching for it I was fully back in my body. Phew! I stared at the stick for a minute and then it hit me. I knew exactly what to write: I AM the Lioness.

OWNING IT ALL

That experience transformed me from the inside out. It reshaped me into the woman I am today. I had chosen at that moment when my totem appeared to merge with her and become one. In accepting the embodi-ment of the lioness, I had to own all the aspects of who she is. This own-ership meant that I had to get comfortable being all her qualities at once: fierceness, independence, loyalty, bravery, strength, and agility. She also had different roles: she was a hunter, a protective mother, and responsible for creating harmony and support within the pride. Lionesses share the responsibility of hunting and raising each other's cubs so that the others can hunt and recover. Thus, they create harmony and strength for their pride. What? They don't work themselves to exhaustion? They allow others to help them? What a concept!

This merging created a profound reorganizing of sorts within my mind, body, and soul. In many aspects, I was already the Lioness. I am the hunter—in modern day terms, the primary provider. I am a mother. I am all those positive qualities. The problem was that until that day, I was not all of those qualities and roles at one time. I was fragmented. I wasn't allowing myself to be a whole person.

I realized I often wore different metaphorical hats at different times to symbolize different roles. Let me explain: each time I put on a hat it defined what character I was supposed to be. If I had my career badass hat on, I fully stepped into that role leaving my role as mother and wife in the background. When I had my mom hat on, I stepped fully into the role of mom and my roles as career badass and wife went to the sidelines. If I had my wife hat on, I stepped out of my role as mom and career badass. Without consciously doing so, I had become a master at compartmentalizing the different roles I played.

While this may have helped me establish my career, this method of dividing myself was destroying me. I felt fragmented, frustrated, and like I was failing at being great at anything. I felt I was the Queen of Mediocre. I was always trying to be some aspect of myself rather than allowing myself to be all of these aspects at the same time. I think it's common for us to feel like we're not good enough when we are trying to be the best parent, assist our kids in distance learning, work our jobs, be a supportive spouse, a present child for our parents, a good friend—we are scrambling at best and lose track of our true selves in this sort of frantic multi-tasking.

It dawned on me that this compartmentalizing was another factor in why things went so south at FTP Travel. I only allowed myself the space to be one role at a time. I never allowed for all of those things to be part of Becca at the same time. This division created a ton of inner conflict, not to mention the fact that I felt like I was being pulled in multiple different directions. Ouch! No wonder my body started to get sick.

In the days and weeks that followed this massive shift of perception, I continued to merge my spirit with the spirit of the Lioness. I felt her message ringing as truth throughout me and everything I did. It was as if there was a whisper from within, reminding me to own the wisdom carried in this message.

"You look too much for guidance outside you. It made you abandon your pride, yourself, and your kids. Embody me. You will question yourself no more and all will be restored."

I was already finding freedom in expressing myself. My confidence had been increasing since my days at FTP Travel. But this little wisdom nugget was the next thing I needed to really rise into my own magnificence. This is what I needed to embody in order to create a life I loved on my own terms. It was at this point that the balancing act became far less precarious and the pieces fell into place with more ease. When we root down into the full essence of who we are, from that space we can rise into the truest version of ourselves. Life expands to support you and things get easier.

This new belief was forming inside me and it was so refreshing! In addition to allowing my most significant roles—career badass, mom, and wife—the space to coexist at the same time, I was also allowing my personal side to emerge. I was an avid self-help junkie, a kundalini teacher, a dedicated yogi and meditator, a writer, a creator, a traveler, and a total personal-transformation nerd. What's weird is that I never allowed these elements of myself to live in the same space as my career.

It's not that I didn't share excitement about these things when I was at work. These things are my passions and they ooze out of me. The difference is that I didn't own these qualities. I sought approval and validation from my bosses and my peers. I felt ashamed about some of these qualities as if they would not be accepted in the corporate setting. It was as if I needed permission to allow these qualities shine through. I needed approval from someone to merge my personal and professional worlds; approval I was never going to get because that approval needed to come from me. Once I realized that I was the one who needed to be giving the stamp of approval, I did so.

What I have learned painfully through experience is that the moment you seek validation from someone else for something, you are rejecting that aspect of yourself. For example, seeking others' approval for showing personal aspects of myself while I was at work was a clear sign that I did not approve of these qualities. These attributes wanted love and acceptance and I was rejecting them.

It became clear that I'm the one who needs to love the good, the bad, and the ugly about myself. To really harness my inner CEO and thrive at the helm of Becca Enterprises, I needed to take ownership of all the self-rejection, negative self-talk, and the seeking of answers outside myself. Ownership doesn't mean fixing it. As in my Beyoncé example, she wasn't the best tennis player but that was just something she needed to make peace with. Her inner diva needed her to own that and move on from tennis and, instead, own her gifts of being one of the greatest singers and performers of all time.

I needed to be okay being a diamond. Diamonds are multifaceted. Some facets are clearer than others, some facets are smaller than others, but that doesn't make one facet better than another. To see the beauty of a diamond, you need to be able to see the sparkling of all the facets. In becoming the diamond, I also needed to own my strengths, roles, and desires and allow them the space to coexist as one. This part was the hardest for me, I had built a fierce habit of rejecting them.

In the other life that I experienced during Sweaty Tribal Sunday, I had proudly displayed my strengths and talents for all to see. Each bracelet meant something. I had them up to my forearms. How cool was that? Can you imagine walking around so comfortable with your strengths and talents that they were publicly displayed? Can you imagine being so comfortable with yourself that you proudly showed who you are to the world?

I made a promise to myself. From that moment on, I was going to honor my gifts and talents. I was going to own that I was multifaceted, I was going to embody multiple roles, and I wasn't going to hide who I was any longer. If it meant that I lost friends, so be it. If I meant I need to find a different place to work, so be it. I was even willing to risk my marriage.

Fortunately, my marriage stayed intact, and I was loving my work at Riverbed so I didn't need to change my job. The only thing I did lose along the way were some friendships, or maybe I haven't lost them, but they have definitely shifted and become less influential in my life. It's all good because this allowed new friendships that support who I am today to enter.

I am now the proud owner of all aspects of myself—the good, the bad, and the ugly. It was at this point that I was able to claim my success and happiness. The power of AND once again came to provide much needed relief. I no longer had to choose success for happiness or happiness for success—I could have both, and that was liberating as hell.

> *Life Hack: You don't have to choose between success and happiness—you can absolutely have both by owning all the aspects of you!*

SUBTLE YET SIGNIFICANT

When the profoundness of a major shift wears off, things feel like they return back to normal. That's the way we're wired. It's not until later reflection that we often realize how significant of a change we made.

Many shifts are subtle and for the most part they go unseen. It's not as though we have a powerful shift and it changes our hair from blonde to green. If it happened that way, every time we looked in the mirror we would be reminded that we'd shifted because we would see our green hair.

Everyone on the outside would see our green hair and know we'd had a major shift.

But that's not how shifts happen. They happen deep on the inside and it takes time for the outer world to catch up. When the intensity of the shift settles and integrates, we go back to our lives. We go back to work, back to the gym, back to our kids, our pets, our weirdness, and we go about our life. It isn't until we're faced with a new opportunity or a new challenge that we have an opportunity to see ourselves rise. We get a chance to see how much we've healed, how much we've grown, and how much we are owning who we really are.

It was now March 2019. Six months had passed since Sweaty Tribal Sunday. I had processed a lot about myself and who I wanted to be, the dust had settled, and I was going about my life. Home life was much better. I had the courage to face my husband about things that had hurt me and our family during the dark years. He had the courage to share his hurt feelings over those years as well. We reconciled and decided to move forward together, giving ourselves permission to unfold into the new versions of ourselves.

We had built our dream home, witnessed the whole building process, and had moved in. It was incredible to have a new space to allow the new energy a place to grow. Our finances were finally in a recovered state after my years at FTP Travel. My anxiety and ADHD were no longer running the show. These were pretty significant changes: they all unfolded one step at a time and, for the most part, felt organic and subtle. There wasn't much stress in the way life was supporting us and it felt fantastic!

While I was relishing this new supportive life that I was living, another opportunity presented itself. I was recruited by Cisco to join their Network Transformation team as a SD-WAN specialist. Now, this might sound like a foreign language to you, but to me it was music to my ears. Working for Cisco had been a dream of mine from my early days in Tech.

I was thriving in my career. I had left leadership after dedicating many years to that career path and was back in the field working with executives at the top enterprise accounts in Florida. Now here I was being recruited by Cisco. I didn't have to do anything to make that happen. It came to me.

I had been in the process of exploring new opportunities outside of Riverbed. I was back on my A game and wanted to see what the market looked like. I was on the edge of accepting an offer with another company when Cisco reached out to me via LinkedIn. I was honest with all parties, and suddenly, with little effort on my end, I had offers from two companies and a counteroffer from Riverbed in my inbox.

I was finally in a position where I was feeling worthy of my success. I felt confident in my skills, gifts, and abilities. I also felt comfortable allowing all my roles and responsibilities to coexist within myself. I was embodying the power of AND—showing up boldly and beautifully in the world. It felt clear that Cisco was the direction that would support me the best.

HELMET CHECK
Decision Breakdown

Making the decision to become a certified kundalini teacher, unbeknownst to me at the time, was one of the best decisions I could have made to heal my past, my trauma, and to invite emotions like ease and joy to the table. As you rise into your role of CEO of your own life, feeling good is part of this experience. It's kind of the whole point. Why go through all these steps to continue to feel like crap? In taking the helm of your enterprise, you get to prioritize yourself and create the vision for your life. If you screw up and make some bad choices, no biggie, choose again.

Old patterns can be hard to break, especially if you have had a traumatic childhood or other events that have shaped you. Your nervous system needs to be retrained so that it's safe to experience ease and joy. Simply put, trauma is a thief of joy.

I was bound and determined not to allow my trauma to control me anymore. I was sick and tired of walking around in high anxiety with scattered thoughts, exhaustion, and overall unhappiness. No matter how much therapy I received or how much I meditated, I couldn't shake the grip that my deepest wounds of losing both my parents had on my life. I definitely have some other large events that I would consider traumatic but those are at the top.

I felt I had no other choice than to study and learn more about it. That's why I signed up for Mastin Kipp's trauma-informed Live Your Purpose coaching certification along with reading whatever I could to understand it better.[23] My life and I both were finally thriving. I wanted to maintain my emotional freedom. I also had an intention to help other people live their best lives too. But, my very first step was to break free from the grips of my past; then I could apply what I learned to help others.

I learned a lot, but there were two elements that really stood out to me in this training and that explain a lot of what occurred on Sweaty Tribal Sunday. The first is that we need to include our bodies in our healing journey, and, secondly, we need to understand what our two primary feel-good emotions are that we are subconsciously seeking to obtain.

In the book *The Body Keeps the Score*, Bessel Van der Kolk, one of the leading trauma experts in the world, shares that—through his studies—he has found that 80 percent of trauma is stored in the body.[24] Unless you release trauma from your body during your healing journey, you are destined to be sabotaged by it.

As I studied trauma, it became more and more clear why, in the previous few years, I had made radical improvements. In addition to implementing all of this book's concepts in my life, I had also consciously connected

23 "Live Your Purpose Certificate Program," Mason Kipp, accessed February 21, 2021, https://mastinkipp.com/lyp-certificate?fbclid=IwAR1lsrEXUI1hmnJoIOlXJPyyw2_a8pSFBODF37-5MhG9u1pTCkJP_UyIBW0.
24 Bessel van der Kolk, *The Body Keeps the Score: Brain, Mind, and Body in the Healing of Trauma* (New York, NY: Penguin, 2015).

with my body as part of my healing experience. This is why it felt like miracle after miracle was appearing in my life. As I came to find out, yoga (all styles), chanting and mantra, emotional freedom technique (tapping), EMDR, acupuncture, mindful walking, breathing exercises, and co-regulation through safe relationships/community were all at the top of the list.

I encourage running and HIIT for overall fitness, and Orangetheory Fitness is my go-to to blow off the amount of stress I carry. I know there are countless stories of healing that have occurred through these intense workout programs (I for one have experienced it), but I want to highlight that in studies for healing trauma, high-intensity workouts aren't included as proven healing modalities to help trauma move up and out of the body.

After understanding some of the results of the studies, I understood why kundalini yoga was transformative and healing for me and for others. It's because it includes the body as part of the many primary ways of removing the nasty grips of trauma. Ultimately, this reorganizing of sorts brings in more ease and less stress because we're able to feel safe in our experiences. The past loosens its grip and control, thus allowing you to experience joy on a more regular basis.

After understanding this, it made me proud to be a kundalini teacher; I had a proven tool in my kit to help my clients and students transform from the inside out. Now I understood that because my body was such an active part of the experience, I was able to embody the Lioness in the depth of my being—allowing her to become part of me.

I understood that rising into the role of CEO of my own life meant I needed to be willing to accept all aspects of myself, and I was finally ready to do so.

PUTTING IT INTO PRACTICE
Step 12: Owning It All
....

Now that we have some context around embodiment and your two primary feel-good emotions, we are going to explore what those emotions are for you. For example, my two primary feel-good emotions are *belonging* and *freedom.*

When I discovered this, my need for approval and validation from the folks at FTP Travel made sense, I wanted to belong. And when I didn't belong, I tried desperately to, so much so that I was unwilling to walk away from a situation that was harming me. It also made sense why I shut down and became small. I wanted the freedom to express myself fully as I am, without being altered. Being asked to be 50 percent of myself was the opposite of freedom, it made me feel caged.

Lastly, everything about the Lioness made sense. The Lioness is free and belongs in the pride. In my tribal past life I reveled in my freedom and belonging. Via that experience of Sweaty Tribal Sunday, I was able to embody those feel-good emotions of freedom and belonging once more and I knew I deserved to experience them regularly.

I realized I didn't need to go searching for table scraps of freedom and belonging when the whole feast was available to me—if I only believed I deserved it. And now I believed it. I was rising into the role of CEO of my own life. I was no longer on the Bridge of In-Between. I had crossed over and was now standing at the helm of my enterprise. That's exactly the shift you are going to make here, starting with identifying your top two feel-good emotions.

Below, I want you to write down all the feel-good emotions you experience as we take a trip back in time. We are going to travel back to a recent feel-good memory and also to a feel-good memory from your childhood.

Then we are going to identify which of all those feel-good emotions you resonate with the most.

Exploring a Recent Feel-Good Memory

I want you to close your eyes and think about a recent feel-good memory. For me, I can easily go back to the birth of both my children, my wedding day with Jermey, or even a recent trip to Universal Studios with just my kids and my niece and nephew. There is no right memory—you can experience any memory that pops up that brings you a sense of feeling good. I want you to think about who is with you? Where are you? And what emotions are you feeling? Write them below:

Who is there? _____

Where are you? _____

What feel-good emotions are you feeling?

_____

_____

Exploring a Feel-Good Childhood Memory

I want you to close your eyes and think about a feel-good memory from childhood. For me, I can easily go back to learning to swing with my dad, being about three and pushing my younger cousin in a baby walker, or even riding in the Zoom-Zoom with my grandma. There is no right memory—you can experience any memory that pops up that brings you a sense of feeling good. I want you to think about who is with you? Where are you? And what emotions are you feeling? Write them below:

Who is there? _____

Where are you? _____

What feel-good emotions were you feeling?

_____

_____

Now that you have completed those two memories, what positive feelings appeared in both?

_____

_____

Pick the two feel-good emotions that resonate for you the most and write them below.

_____

_____

How have you searched and longed to receive these emotions with the wrong people and situations?

_____

_____

How are you embodying these emotions today in a way that supports you?

_____

_____

Note: For a deeper dive into this topic, reference Mastin Kipp's Book, *Claim Your Power.*

EXERCISE
Metaphorical Hats
. . . .

Now that we have an idea of some of the emotions that help you feel connected and alive inside, let's identify all the metaphorical hats you wear. The idea here is to help you understand the different roles you play. From there, we will look at how we can integrate them into the wholeness of who you are, rather than compartmentalizing.

If we relate this back to the theme of an enterprise, the CEO is responsible for the entire organization. The moment the CEO title was accepted, there would be no more managing of operations through the lens of a singular department. This is precisely what is happening to you. With your rise into the role of CEO of your own life, you are removing the lens of singularity and looking at things holistically.

Below, list at least five different metaphorical hats that you wear—full permission to write more than five if you want!

Example: mom, career badass, daughter, distant-learning teacher assistant, self-help junkie, yogi, etc.

1.

2.

3.

4.

5.

After writing down your different roles, explain how you compartmentalize these roles currently.

_____

_____

After learning that allowing all roles to be part of you at all times is best for your overall wellness and ability to thrive, what areas of your life can you begin to change?

_____

_____

What did you find most insightful about the exercise and concept of allowing yourself to be multifaceted?

_____

_____

How do you plan to incorporate your body into the rise of your role to break those troublesome patterns?

_____

_____

You can return to the exercise anytime at: https://www.beccapowers. com/worksheetshyic

| KATE

I met Kate the same way I met Vanessa, through the Women's Prosperity Network. Nancy Matthews, the founder, is phenomenal at connecting people and knew we should all get to know each other. Kate was very much like Vanessa in the sense that she had a larger-than-life spark to her. I just knew she was destined for greatness. Kate has a smile that lights up a room and I believe she always sensed that success and happiness were meant to be embraced at the same time—and she owned it. I believe she understood back then, in 2008, that having both—success and happiness—did not require you to sacrifice one or the other: a lesson that took me several years to understand.

Kate has always been involved heavily in the local community. She is a natural at connecting people, resources, and businesses to help them succeed with more ease. She is a gifted writer, content creator, and marketer. And on top of those things she is an avid reader and an advocate of other people's work. She is always using her own platform to inspire and influence entrepreneurs, small businesses, and the community as a whole, to share the wisdom she gains in a way that helps others embrace their own success, happiness, and all their fabulous qualities.

Kate is able to maintain a pretty sustainable zone of success and happiness because she embraces her wholeness and her gifts; she knows that physical fitness, yoga, creative projects, and connecting with other like-minded individuals is what her soul needs to feel alive and well. This aliveness inspires her to create the meaningful content and programs that she does regardless of the role she is in. Kate has created multiple podcasts, with one currently in production; she is the co-host of "Create for No Reason," and she has been the video host of two shows, one with GoDaddy and one for Delray Beach, Florida.

Like Connie, Kate is one who dances with the Universe. From the outside looking in, it feels like Kate understands the Universe's whispers of opportunity and she is able to say "yes" when opportunities present themselves. Coming from this secure place, where success and happiness have permission to coexist, Kate's curiosity, willingness to connect with others, and desire to build strong relationships is a good representation of what harnessing your inner CEO looks like when the internal system works well.

One example of Kate's cosmic dances with the Universe in action is how she became CEO. Kate has had a pretty awesome career in business development as a small business marketing strategist and content creator. Kate had recently read the book *The Dream Manager* by Matthew Kelly. Feeling moved by the book and knowing that its content would inspire others, she reached out to the author. The initial correspondence was to see if he would be able to speak at an event. Matthew said "yes" and they began to get to know each other a little. As I mentioned, Kate is a natural at building strong relationships and I wasn't surprised to learn that they had stayed in touch, but I *was* surprised and in complete awe when Kate stepped into the role of CEO of Floyd Consulting, Matthew Kelly's consulting firm. All of her hard work both within herself and within her career had paid off as the most beautiful expression of a woman honoring her magnificence.

Kate, of course, like every other human, has her challenges and adversities. The difference is they don't define her. She allows the Power of AND to exist within her daily life and therefore is able to express her success AND happiness without sacrificing herself. Kate has not only harnessed her inner CEO but her outer one as well because she is not afraid to share her gifts with the world. How empowering is that!

13 / TURN PAIN INTO PURPOSE

*"Adversity introduces a woman t
o herself and her power."*

—Unknown

THE ROLLER COASTER

By this point, I felt pretty confident that life was more like a roller coaster than any other analogy I could think of. Reflecting back on my journey, it was filled with ups and down, loops, spirals, speed, terrifying climbs, and exhilarating falls. Sometimes it's been like riding on "The Everest" at Disney's Animal Kingdom, where, unexpectedly, I'd feel like I was about to fly off the tracks and then get pulled backwards a bit before the ride got back on track. And yet, regardless of what part of my life I was experiencing, I realized I was always progressing forward just as on a real roller coaster.

I also knew that I had a choice. I had the option of riding the roller coaster of life with my eyes squeezed shut, clutching the bars for dear life, and fearing that I might die. Or, I could open my eyes and look forward with curiosity, holding the bars for support as I leaned into the experience, and feeling just how alive I am as I experience the thrill of the ride. As I considered the options, I decided on the latter.

I also became increasingly aware that I wasn't going to be able to see every twist and turn that was coming my way: Perhaps right when I thought things were going smoothly, there'd be another incline that I'd have to choose whether to clinch or embrace. What I certainly didn't have awareness of until I experienced these final stories I'm about to share with you, is that oftentimes the ride ends right where it began. Then it begins again with a fresh new perspective.

As I take you into these final stories, I want to preface that in my typical roller-coaster lifestyle, life offers experiences that weren't planned—and I choose to embrace them with openness and curiosity. And for you, my fellow CEO, you have one more magic carpet ride and one more painful part of my past to experience with me before our journey ends. This would be a good time to read forward with curiosity, hold the bars for support as you lean into the experience, and feel just how alive you can be when you embrace the very thing you've been closing your eyes to. I hope my final story inspires you to choose to begin your next ride on *your* roller coaster of life with a fresh new perspective. Sometimes our greatest pain can become our greatest purpose.

HOLDING HANDS

It was November, one month past Sweaty Tribal Sunday, when I was overtaken by a longing to connect with my parents. So much had transpired in October with the depth of my healing and awakening that I had barely taken a moment to honor their death anniversaries, which were also in October. I wanted so badly to call them to discuss everything I had been through and that I'd realized about my life—our life.

Knowing that yoga and meditation are the best ways for me to connect with the part of me that is always connected to them, I had signed up for a guided chakra meditation and healing session with a locally acclaimed healer named Joseph LoBrutto III. I had seen the event on Facebook and I had heard good things about him, so I decided to give it a shot.

I drove to one of my favorite local crystal shops, Spiritual Journey in Coral Springs, where the workshop was being hosted. The crazy thing about this location is that it's about five minutes from where I grew up. I learned how to drive my mom's manual 1987 Ford Mustang on the very street that's behind the shop! The other unique aspect of this location is that it is right next to Yoga Source—my kundalini yoga home studio. I find it awesome that my two primary yoga and meditation healing centers are right next to each other on the very street where I learned to drive—small world considering I now live 45 minutes north of that area.

When I arrived at Spiritual Journey, the shop owner, Barbara, greeted me as I walked past the wide array of different colored crystals, incense, and fairy figurines to the back room where all the workshops are held. I grabbed an open seat and began to relax to the soft meditation music in the background. A few minutes later, Joseph walked in, did his intro, and began to lead us through a guided meditation of each of the chakra centers. Each chakra represents a specific area of life, and I could feel my energy moving. When I reached a strong meditative state I felt a slight humming or vibration in my body. This was my signal that I was in the zone. Thirty minutes later—which felt like five minutes—Joseph began to wrap up the guided meditation. My energy was calm and clear. Just the reset I needed.

Unexpectedly, Joseph continued the workshop rather than wrapping it up. He shifted gears from our chakras to a more esoteric experience. I was feeling a bit confused because I was about to pull myself out of the meditative trance that he had put us in. I took a deep breath and allowed myself to continue with the experience, returning to the humming sensation. Joseph asked us to envision the gates of heaven. He said, "Here you have an opportunity to say hello to a deceased loved one. When I guide you to the open gates, your deceased loved one, who's longing to connect with you, will walk through the gates."

A few tears began to fall down my face and my heart started racing. I was hoping one of my parents would walk through in this most unexpected visualization exercise. I tried to shake off any expectations so I wouldn't be disappointed if nothing happened, but I was eager for something to happen—hopeful that I would have a visualization with at least one of my parents.

When the gates opened, I was shocked in delight. Through the gates walked my mom and dad, holding hands. It had been almost 20 years since I had seen them together. Joseph guided us to greet them. Mom and Dad greeted me with a hug. I needed that hug the same way I needed the eight-armed hug from Mother Kali back in 2014. I was so overjoyed and overwhelmed that I practically pulled myself out of the experience. Luckily, I was able to keep with the visualization and receive that long overdue embrace.

Joseph asked our deceased loved ones to present us with a gift. My mom took the lead and presented me with a guardian angel named Sarah. It made me laugh that her name was Sarah because of my mom's obsession with Fleetwood Mac, which recorded a song named "Sara." My mom had successfully passed the Fleetwood Mac/Stevie Nicks obsession down to me.

A few minutes later, Joseph wrapped up the workshop—for real this time. I was smiling ear to ear. Not only did I get my chakras balanced but I got to see my parents holding hands, I received a hug, and I got a freakin' guardian angel—I considered that event a success!

HER NAME IS SARAH

A couple of months later, in February 2019, I was headed back to Coral Springs for my Saturday kundalini class with one of the master teachers. Since Sweaty Tribal Sunday, I'd been trying to keep my yoga practice consistent, to allow time for the depth of that experience to integrate with my mind, body, and soul. Spiritual Journey, being next door, offers a little shopping temptation after class. I had thought that I would probably pop in and say hello to everyone there after class—maybe buy some new crystals. I mean, what are the odds that my home yoga studio is next to a crystal shop? A yogi's dream come true!

I arrived, parked my Durango, and began to walk to my yoga class. As I got closer, I noticed that Spiritual Journey had their door propped open. It was decorated with a large sign and balloons. Curious what was going on, I finally got close enough to see—they were having a psychic fair. Since the chakra workshop, where I had the visualization of my mom and dad holding hands, I had become more open to the idea of psychics. After that workshop, I had come to the conclusion that healing from deep grief looks different for everyone. I was healing and making positive progress with the alternative arts, and I was honoring that space for myself. Perhaps, for me, it took wild and abstract experiences to feel connected to my parents and to relieve some of the sorrow I'd been carrying around for years. The possibility of releasing more pent up grief was very appealing. Plus, I love trying new things. I thought, "What the heck!" and signed up for a mini psychic session. It would start about 15 minutes after yoga class. I walked into yoga curious what this mini-reading experience would bring.

Class was excellent as always. I have never done another style of yoga that allows me to connect so deeply with myself. Sometimes it really does make me feel like I've been taking drugs because it gives me a wonderful high, but the beauty is, I'm 100 percent sober and I created this buzz all by myself. I left Yoga Source feeling connected not only to myself but also to everything else around me.

I arrived back at Spiritual Journey and met with Theresa. Theresa is a gifted medium and I had heard good things about her, which helped me lower my guard. It didn't take me long to ground myself with the opening breath exercises, because I had just spent 90 minutes doing breathwork in kundalini. I think that taking the yoga class prior to this session set me up for another unexpected cosmic experience—another magic carpet ride.

Theresa began the reading by saying that my dad would like to come through and was asking my permission to move forward. I acknowledged that I wanted to hear more—I was curious what Theresa was going to say. She confirmed various things so I knew for sure it was him. I validated that what she was telling me was true. She went on to say, "He's with one of your…oh…ohhh…I don't know how to say this. Have you lost a child?"

"No," I answered, "I haven't."

"I don't mean to pry," she said, "but did you choose to terminate a pregnancy?"

A tear began to fall slowly down my face and my stomach began to turn. I had forgotten. How could I have forgotten? The shame rose up along with the pain as I replied, "Yes, I did. When I was 17."

Theresa offered me a tissue along with an amazing amount of compassion. She extended her arms and offered me a small embrace. She said, "Your dad is with her and says she's doing great. They are the best of buds. He wants you to know her name is Sarah."

At this point, I was frozen in a flood of information and memories. My tears turned from tears of sadness to comfort, knowing she was with my dad. If we are souls—which I do believe—there is no better place Sarah can be than with my dad. He was always the best with children. And it made all the more sense to me that my mom had told me my guardian angel was named Sarah just a couple of months earlier.

Theresa asked me, "Would you like to hear from Sarah? She has a message for you." I nodded "yes" as I could barely breathe, let alone speak. Theresa said, "Sarah wants you to know you don't have to feel guilty about the decision you made. Her soul was not intended to have a full gestation period and you would have lost the pregnancy. She wants you to know that she knows you loved her and that it was a very hard decision for you. She knows that it left you with an extreme amount of pain, shame, and guilt. She has witnessed the burden you have been carrying around for over two decades. She gives you permission to let it all go. She says she knows she has a brother and sister and has been watching over them since they were born. Sarah wants me to tell you that she loves you and wishes that you weren't so sad and ashamed."

Theresa paused for a second just to check in and make sure I was doing okay before continuing. "Sarah has one more message for you. She wants you to share your story. She says so many women suffer over their choice to terminate a pregnancy, and so many suffer when a pregnancy is unexpectedly lost. Our souls picked you to be our mom because we knew you would be strong enough to carry us and to love us as we resolved our karma in the womb. We don't want our chosen moms to suffer. Can you let others know that their soul babies are always with them and cheering them on?"

I nodded through my sobs.

My 15 minutes of a mini session were over. Theresa handed me another tissue and gave me another hug. She embraced me the same way a mother would. She held me for a few seconds and said, "Now, now. Your baby is with you."

DIFFICULT DECISION

Making the decision to terminate my pregnancy had been the single most difficult and shameful act I have had to live with. I don't mean shameful in a way that I wish I could reverse my decision. I mean shameful in the way I was never able to express how much I was hurting after the choice was made—without feeling shamed by society. I was only 17. I used protection but still somehow got pregnant. I remember feeling scared, confused, helpless, and powerless. I remember feeling alone. I had no one to turn to, no one to comfort me, and no one to offer a path of healing. So, at 17 I shoved it down inside as far as it could go. It was so far down that—in trauma language—I disassociated from that memory until I was present enough with myself, 20 years later, that I was willing to recognize that this surfaced memory needed a safe place to be healed.

From my experience and from talking to other women who have lost babies—by choice or not—we all concur that part of us is never the same afterward. These feelings I experienced of shame, sadness, longing, helplessness, powerlessness, and even defectiveness are all feelings shared by women who have lost their babies. These feelings, carried over prolonged periods of time, disempower our beingness.

Sarah's message that our babies are always with us, that they chose us, and that they were able to resolve the karma all because we were able to love them in the womb is very powerful. This message can help relieve women of the deep pain that they have endured. And although the message was delivered to the moms from Sarah's perspective, I feel this message is important for the dads that have lost their babies too.

It is my hope that in the vulnerable sharing of my story that Sarah provides a pathway for others to heal—to restore their wholeness. And for those suffering from a loss of an unborn baby to be embraced by their family and friends. I hope that women who have to make this difficult decision can feel supported enough to have a safe place to grieve and receive the comfort they need.

I hope the women who've tried to conceive several times but can't make it to full-term feel a sense of wholeness: that they can ask for support and receive it with their head and hearts held high. I hope the dads that have experienced the loss can get the support they need to feel strong and heal. I hope that society as a whole can start to recognize the pain that is associated with the loss of an unborn baby, and that we—as in society—can begin to embrace each other rather than reject each other. And lastly, if you have lost an unborn baby, I hope that you can, at minimum, embrace yourself and give yourself permission to feel whole and complete. You deserve the gift of self-love rather than self-suffering.

A MAGICAL SYNCHRONICITY

If you are skeptical, that's okay. I will be the first one to admit I don't have the concept of life beyond this one fully figured out. What I *can* say is the experience was real and offered many synchronicities and enough validation for me to experience it as real. And for the purpose of healing a 20-year-old grief, it was exactly the experience I needed to begin that process. I had connected with my daughter. She had a name, Sarah. She was with my dad. Her story continued. It didn't end. Since that day, I have been open about my choice to terminate the pregnancy. I share her story and her message with the hope that it helps other wounded women heal.

I talk to Sarah now, the same way I talk to my mom and my dad. I do believe she is one of my guardian angels. Here is an example of her guiding me since our reunion in Feb 2019: I was terrified about taking this manuscript to an editor. Due to my original wound being centered on the fact that I was punished for expressing myself authentically—and that same wound was recently reopened at FTP Travel back in 2014—my nervous system did everything possible to delay sending off the manuscript you are reading now.

I needed to get clear and unstuck fast, otherwise my dreams would die in the arms of my perceived fear. I had stepped out of my power and I knew it. I returned to the first four steps in this book. Then prayed about it to the Universe, my mom, my dad, and Sarah. I finally got the courage to schedule a call with the editing-pairing services. We interviewed each other. Afterward, the gentleman who was doing the pairing said, "I have someone in mind who I think will be a perfect fit for this book. I will reach out to her and see if she's interested. If so, I will introduce you in an email."

A day later I had an email from the editing service that said in the opening line:

"Becca, I'd like to introduce you to your editor, Sarah."

The Universe and Sarah had given me my breadcrumb.

TURNING PAIN INTO PURPOSE

I wanted to share this as the last story because our greatest pain surfaces, ready to be healed, when we step into our becoming—and I want you prepared for that. We think the healing is done and—boom—that pesky shadow pops up because we are ready to look at the pain and fear without rejecting them. We are ready to give them space to heal, be forgiven, and to integrate wholeness back into our lives. It's as if the shadow knows we have the tools and strength to finally face it.

Facing this shadow memory is one of the hardest things I've ever had to do. Talking about it openly is even harder. What embracing this story—wholly—has helped me understand, is that our pain can be turned into purpose. Every lesson I share in this book has been a result of a perspective shift and the willingness to turn my pain to purpose. That purpose for me is sharing my stories of rising above the pain so that others can use them as a source of inspiration to rise above their own pain.

I have seen that each time I've shared one of my stories, it has helped someone else to heal. Each time I see someone else heal, I heal a little more. Each time I heal a little more, the more cemented I am as the CEO of my life. I am positioned to harness my inner CEO and live a life I love by not rejecting myself anymore.

Here's an example of turning pain into purpose as it relates to this story. I was at an entrepreneurial workshop with a friend. We were split into different groups. During the breakout session, my friend had come face to face with the pain that was associated with the choice to terminate a pregnancy. After our breakout sessions, she couldn't stop the tears falling from her eyes. She told me she would fill me in after the event when we got in the car.

On the way home, she shared with me that she had to make a difficult decision when she was younger to terminate a pregnancy. She mentioned that she hadn't told very many people out of fear. I shared with her my experience of learning about Sarah and the things Theresa shared with me. Hearing that our babies are still with us and that they are doing well brought a smile to her face, but I could sense that part of her was skeptical too. I understood—the story is pretty far out.

She asked if we could stop by Publix to grab a bottle of wine, and as we walked into the store, Fleetwood Mac's song "Sara" was playing through the loudspeaker. My friend started to cry, grabbed me for a big hug and said, "Thank you. I mean seriously thank you."

Our deepest pain and the things we feel the most shame about often contain our biggest gifts. When we let the Universe in and shed light on them, something incredible happens: the Grinch Effect goes into action and our very essence expands—times three. We become a beacon of light for others. We step into our becoming and our pain becomes purpose.

For me, my deepest pain was rejecting myself and my actions over and over again. I rejected my gifts and talents. I rejected my wounds. I sought all my validation and approval from others—which I was never going to receive until I approved of myself. My pain turned to purpose when I started to accept myself, flaws and all. My pain turned into purpose when I allowed myself to be a human worthy of greatness, success, love, compassion, and prosperity.

That is the gift I hope to give to you. I hope that throughout this book you have come to learn and believe that you matter. That your life is precious. That you deserve to have a life you love. That you have the freedom to create a life you love on your terms—not someone else's. Yes, there is a place for collaboration if you are in a relationship and/or caring for others. *But*—if you don't love yourself, approve of yourself, and accept yourself—faults and all—it's very likely you will put others before yourself and continue to live with anxiety, fear, and being unfulfilled.

When you can turn your pain to purpose, you will remain the CEO of your enterprise. You will find yourself honoring all the aspects of yourself that give you much more energy and ease. You are no longer wasting time or energy trying to hide things, balance things, overcorrect things. There is much more space to let things be as they are, and from that space you will rise into the fullness of your potential.

Life Hack: Your pain turns to purpose when you accept yourself, flaws and all.

HARNESSING YOUR INNER CEO

As I took on the role of CEO of my own life, I found that self-acceptance helped me keep it simple. I could work at Cisco and accept myself. I could write a book and accept myself. I could royally screw up and accept myself. My purpose is no longer tied to an ideal or another person. I have learned that is a recipe for disaster and takes me much further away from my life thriving. I now understand that I am constantly evolving and to cut myself a break if I need one.

As I close out our experience together, I wanted to share with you a few successes I've had since I harnessed my inner CEO. I have no problem speaking up for myself, saying "no" when I mean "no," and prioritizing my needs and my health first. As a result, my autoimmune is in remission and I have lost 20 pounds. My goal is to reverse the autoimmune disease altogether and take daily steps in that direction.

I'm feeling joy on a more regular basis, which is a fantastic change. I am driven as hell, but I find that I'm allowing possibilities 10 times more than pushing them. I am enjoying richness and health in my relationships. My coaching and speaking business has grown while I guide others to the place where they are experiencing success and happiness. I had the best year of my sales career at Cisco. And even with all that, I have more restorative down time than I've ever had in my life. Nothing had to be sacrificed—everything was able to expand.

Oh, and I make damn sure I get paid my worth. From a monetary perspective, I am now earning four times—if not more—than I was earning at FTP Travel. And to think that just five years ago, I stressed to make ends meet, I was begging to be validated by my employer, and I was going through the darkest years of my life.

Today couldn't be more different than then. Today I am experiencing more success and happiness than I ever dreamed possible—and if I can do it, you can do it too.

PUTTING IT INTO PRACTICE
Step 13: Turn Pain into Purpose
. . . .

The steps in this book are meant for you to come back to over and over again. There is no end to the game called life until we take our last breath. We will run into challenges, triggers, people who piss us off, and people who make us question ourselves. Be prepared for that. When it happens, return to the steps in this book and prioritize yourself. You always have that choice.

In this chapter, we discussed turning pain into purpose. And in this final chapter, you are the CEO, which means that your pain and fear is no longer the boss—you are. In putting this lesson into practice, we are going to look at turning your pain into purpose, helping you remain CEO of your enterprise.

Can you identify a few areas in your life where you can turn your pain into purpose?

Pain into Purpose: First list one pain, then write how you might be able to turn it into purpose.

_____

_____

Pain into Purpose: First list one pain, then write how you might be able to turn it into purpose.

_____

_____

Pain into Purpose: First list one pain, then write how you might be able to turn it into purpose.

_____

_____

Now that you are CEO of your life, how do you foresee being able to remain at the helm when life throws its curveballs? What will you do to ensure you stay there?

_____

_____

EXERCISE

Commitment Statement

. . . .

There is a power in writing things down to affirm them. I have written a commitment statement that I would like you to rewrite with your information in it. I have provided a space below my commitment statement where you can write this same statement in your own handwriting.

I (first name, last name), officially accept my role as CEO of (first name) Enterprises. In this role, I give myself permission to put myself first. I understand that for my enterprise to be healthy and prosperous, this is a must. I am willing to admit when things are fucked. I am willing to reach out to my fan club for support. I am willing to in-

vest and devote time to my executive dream team of advisors because I am worth it.

To all the humans who come into contact with (first name) Enterprises, I solemnly swear to love and accept myself. I commit to creating a life I love on my own terms so that, together, we can thrive. I understand that you thrive when I thrive. The best is yet to come!

Your CEO,

Sign your name

Write this above statement below using your information to fill in the blanks. *Don't even think about skipping this step.* Your future self needs you to do this!

MONICA

Monica is by far one of my favorite people on the planet and she's been very inspirational to me. As I'm sure you've picked up on through the number of times I've referenced her throughout this book, Monica is an introvert by nature. She is an observer and has taught me on more than one occasion to "practice the pause" before acting. And, with my fiery personality, I have needed that reminder on more than one occasion.

Monica, coming from this place of introspection, harnesses her inner CEO differently than I do.

She grew up in South Florida in a city called Hialeah. She is Cuban and first generation American. Her mom and dad came over from Cuba without much of anything besides their skills. Her parents worked hard to put a roof over their heads. Times were often stressful, which meant that Monica, a curious creator by nature, wasn't really allowed to express herself fully without being hushed. There were a couple reasons for this.

One reason was rooted in the Cuban culture—the parents are in charge and kids need to follow the hierarchy. The second reason was more tragic. When Monica was 9 years old, her mom was diagnosed with breast cancer. There wasn't much room for Monica to rock the boat with her opinions and ideas, so she kept them inside as so many of us do. Our stories, ideas, and beliefs get silenced when there isn't a safe place to express them. Her mom, Miriam, passed away from cancer when Monica was 18 years old.

The hushing led to feelings of being unheard, invisible, and small for Monica, and losing her mom led to feelings of being alone, not understood, and lost. So, for Monica to make big and bold moves in her adulthood meant that she had gone through the process of rising into her CEOness—working though default coping mechanisms, old stubborn beliefs, and overall fear—and thus finding a way to turn her pain to purpose.

When we met back in 1999, Monica was, and still is, a licensed mar-riage-family therapist. She was working for other practices but had wanted to open her own private practice. I was impressed as I watched her build her practice from scratch, which ended up being super successful. The events from her childhood made her want to help people, and she thought that being a therapist was a way to make that impact. Monica has an incredible ability to listen, help others find their voice, and step into their confidence so they can have that freedom and liberation she desired for others.

Despite her success, Monica felt very unfulfilled. I remember for years how she would fantasize about leaving it all behind to go to New York. It sounded a little crazy and totally up my alley! I was right in her corner saying she should do it, though part of me didn't think she would because she was so rooted in South Florida. I knew that she had all these roles and responsibilities to tend to.

With Monica's mom passing away, she focused more on her dad. She felt like she would be a bad daughter if she moved away. Her brother was also close to her, and she was really attached to being an aunt. On top of that, she was the owner of a private practice with a list of clients, and her two best friends were local as well. She felt guilt about closing her practice and leaving her clients to find new therapists. She knew her friendships would be fine but having them so accessible was hard to walk away from.

She was living a completely compartmentalized life and was feeling in-creasingly frustrated and unfulfilled. The more frustrated and unfulfilled she felt, the greater the idea of New York captivated her. The thing was, she had to break through the fear of leaving her dad behind. She had already sacrificed her dream of going to Florida State University and stayed local in South Florida by attending Nova Southeastern University. Moving to New York really stretched her.

After months of feeling like a hypocrite, telling her clients that they needed to live their dreams, she realized she wasn't living hers. She was feeling exhausted in her private practice and knew that she was putting the needs of everyone else before her dreams. Monica finally decided to follow her own advice and said, "I'm moving to New York." She was no longer willing to sacrifice her happiness simply for the success of her private practice—she knew she could have both happiness and success. She knew she could move to New York and still be a good daughter, aunt, and friend. She was networked enough to know she could find all of her clients new therapists and that they would be fine. She needed to express two of her feel-good emotions: freedom and adventure

I was so excited for her. I was also bummed that one of my best friends was moving, but this wasn't about me. Her soul needed this, she knew it and I knew it. She was confident in her ability and skill. She knew she would find a job and she did. She lived in a tiny apartment on the Upper East Side of Manhattan. Some months were hard on her financially, but she made it work all the same.

I remember her telling me that she was going to meet her husband soon. I was like, "How do you know that?" She said, "I just know." That "know-ingness" is so powerful and she was tuned into it. And—wouldn't you know—within three months she met her now husband, Gary.

In living a life she loves, Monica often spends time alone to tend to her soul. I don't mean in a way that causes her great depression. I mean giving herself a break from all the noise and bullshit from the outside world so she can tend to her inner world. By doing so she was able to embrace another facet. She is a fantastic fiction/fantasy writer and finally decided to write a book.

She often writes tales of olden days when men and women lived among the fairies and other magical creatures. She beautifully interweaves modern day and other lifetimes where magic existed. She uses both the professional training and experiences she had while studying past life regressions under Dr. Brian Weiss to create the most marvelous stories. The stories are filled with life lessons, unity, and love. It amazes me to see her own all her aspects and this is why I wanted to write about her here in this section.

Monica's enterprise looks much different from mine. For Monica, her career is secondary to her needs for downtime, creativity, time with nature, and, of course, time with her husband. They love the finer things in life like wines, cheese, five-star restaurants, and travel.

Now in her mid 40s, her priorities have shifted. Don't get me wrong, she would be ecstatic to win a million dollars, but money isn't her number one priority. Earning multiple six figures and creating thriving businesses are not at the top of her list like they are for me. Her passions come in the form of enjoying the arts and different experiences the world has to offer. She is happy working her corporate job as a utilization case manager, it gives her the freedom to work from home and she enjoys the balance it provides.

Feeling prosperous and happy is more than just earning money—it's about the quality of life you get to enjoy. Monica reminds me that everything isn't always about goals and achievement. She reminds me there's a joy in sitting still and experiencing the beauty that life has to offer. She reminds me to slow down and savor all flavors of life. This slowing down, breathing, and connecting to life and nature is one surefire way to break free from the grips of trauma—and Monica mastered this one.

Monica is CEO of her own life—on her own terms—and that is what this book is about. Understanding what makes you feel good and at ease allows you to experience abundance in a way that is meaningful to you. Monica, for me, illustrates that there are different ways to turn your pain to purpose, that making difficult decisions is hard but worth it, and that being CEO of your own life will look different for each and every person.

Today Monica is harnessing her inner CEO. Although she wasn't chasing six figures she certainly found it in her pursuit for a more fulfilled life. Today she and Gary have built a brand-new home in the Charlotte area of North Carolina. Standing on her back patio offers a view of a forest with breathtaking sunsets and the sound of running water.

CONCLUSION

I want you to have luscious dreams, lofty goals, and juicy desires. I want you to feel prosperous, happy, whole, and successful. As long as you are breathing, it is your birthright to have your cake and eat it too! Own it. Feel it. Harness your inner CEO. Stand at the helm of your enterprise and feel confident being its leader.

It's important to reinforce that life is life, meaning that you will come across setbacks and you will have breakthroughs. When setbacks happen, return to this book. These steps are proven to get you unstuck, back on track, and embracing your success and happiness—all at the same time.

Let's review your path to CEO:

Part 1: Power: Steps to Claim Your Power

1. Assess the health of your enterprise and begin your journey of expansion.

2. Admit when things are fucked and invite in possibility.

3. Activate your self-worth and begin to honor yourself first.

4. Own where you are to create new opportunities.

Part 2: Passion: Steps to Claim Your Passion

1. Find your fire and ignite the joy that comes from the flames of passion being fanned.

2. Review the relationships in your life and whether or not they support you.

3. Honor the space in-between—the old and the new.

4. Live from the power of AND rather than the diminishing of OR.

5. Create new beliefs that support what you love and the direction of your desire.

Part 3: Prosperity: Steps to Claim Your Prosperity

1. Embrace your self-worth to increase your net worth.

2. Build and evolve your executive dream team for mentorship in the direction of your dreams.

3. Remember, to own all your qualities—the good, the bad, the ugly—especially the good.

4. Turn your pain to purpose and live free.

THE DUALITY THAT IS US

We are both souls and human beings.

For my fellow soul searchers, it's important to remember that we are human beings having a spiritual experience and spiritual beings having a human experience—we're both. No matter how much we may be souls, we cannot bypass our human experiences. We still feel pain that we have to deal with, and we cannot simply manifest it away. We have trauma in our bodies that prevents us from reaching our purest potential if it's not healed. When it's not healed, a level of discontent will always exist. Using phrases like "things happen for reason" or "it is what it is"—although these can be powerful—we bypass our humanness if we use them in the wrong context. Connect with your pain. Honor it. Respect it. Move it. But, please don't dismiss it as if it doesn't exist. Eventually our bodies will express that something needs to resolved by showing up as gut-health issues, anxiety, stress, depression, chronic fatigue, suicide, drug addiction, and more. The steps in this book will help you connect with your humanness so your soul can express its full potential as you turn your pain to purpose. Lastly, it's completely acceptable for spiritual folks to be healthy and wealthy—go out there and claim it!

For my fellow success-driven rockstars, we are also souls having a human experience. We are not robots expected to perform day after day. We are meant to live a life with meaning. There is a great big Universe with tons of energy waiting to support you. We are more than just our bodies. When we ignore our gut feelings and cut off our intuition, our bodies tell us something is wrong. When we are not honoring our magnificence, just as above, our bodies will show us this in gut-health issues, anxiety, stress, depression, chronic fatigue, suicide, drug addiction, and more. Our souls are crying out to be nourished, loved, and expressed. Listen to these whispers from your soul that your needs are not being met. People pleasing and working yourself to death are not the answers. You deserve to be in touch with your creativity, passion, joy—and success. Go out into the world and embrace your AND!

My hope is that this book will help you honor your soul as well as your humanness, and that the stories, steps, and exercises have helped connect you to your wholeness, worth, wealth, and well-being. You have the tools now to harness your inner CEO and live a life you love—like a boss.

PUTTING IT INTO PRACTICE

You are now CEO of your enterprise. Congrats!!! I have a very special certificate to make your promotion official. Please visit https://www.beccapowers.com/ceocertificate to get your gift of completion.

You have everything you need to Harness Your Inner CEO. I look forward to hearing about your wins and successes. Follow me on LinkedIn, Instagram, Facebook, and Clubhouse @beccapowers1313, tag me, and use #harnessyourinnerCEO to share your stories. I can't wait to see them!

AFTERWORD

As the Universe would have it, opportunity came knocking on my door shortly after I completed the writing of this book. During the final round of editing, I got a call from a gentleman named Brian Hill, regional direc-

tor for Fortinet—a rapidly growing cybersecurity company in the tech industry. I knew Brian well because Fortinet's job offer was the one I turned
down in March 2019 when I chose to go to Cisco. When I declined that
offer, I told Brian I believed I *would* work for him one day and that I'd love
to stay in touch. We did—touching base every now and then.

I didn't think much about it when he called in February of this year,
2021, though I could tell by the tone of his voice that this call was different. He had a new job offer for me. As you know by now, I'm always one
to explore possibilities. So, I listened.

One of Brian's top performers had recently been promoted. The sales
territory was local to where I live—meaning no more airplanes and long
trips. It was a mature patch of Fortune 500 and Fortune 1000 accounts.
Additionally, it offered the potential of earning seven-figures—based on
my performance, of course. Although the seven-figure earners were among
the few elite, the possibility was there. And, for me, there only needs to
be that sliver of possibility in the direction of my desire for me to say yes.

Much of what Brian was saying aligned with my next set of goals: working closer to home with less travel (I'd have more time available for the
launch of this book); earning seven-figures; expanding my expertise into
cybersecurity; and working for a tech company where the market was indicating rapid growth. Side note, I'd always worked for well-established
companies that were super successful and on the other side of their big
breakthrough moment in the market. I hadn't yet worked for a company
that was on the brink of market domination, and I wanted that experience on my résumé. Yet even with all those things considered, my initial
response was loaded with severe hesitation: I loved my job at Cisco. I was
successful, I was supported, I was having fun, and I was at Cisco. "Who
leaves Cisco?" was the first thought that went through my head.

With that thought in mind, I declined exploring the offer with Fortinet
any further. But I continued to ruminate on it, remembering one of my
own sayings, "When things are good—great is waiting around the cor-

ner." I decided to embrace my Admit When Things Are Fucked Method. I now know that AWTAF supports so much more than just the situations where you feel stuck in a negative pattern. I've learned that it supports you when you're considering possibilities that are in the direction of your desires, but you're faced with indecision. I needed to get out of my head and into my heart.

I followed the AWTAF Method steps outlined in chapter 2.

- Step 1: **Willingness to admit** there is a problem and that you don't have control over other people, places, and things.

- Step 2: **Believing in possibility**—that there is an outcome you have not considered that supports you better.

- Step 3: **Giving the Universe permission** to intercede and bring in new possibilities that align with an outcome that supports your highest and greatest good and the highest and greatest good of others.

- Step 4: **Following the breadcrumbs** the Universe sends you.

The answer wasn't clear; I wanted both opportunities and knew I could only choose one. I was willing to admit that I needed clarity and that I was faced with indecision. I believed the answer that supported the direction of my desires would arrive to me clearly if I allowed it the space to do so. Next, I gave the Universe permission to intercede and bring the answer that supports me in the highest and greatest good for myself and the highest and greatest good for all. Lastly, I followed the breadcrumbs the Universe sent.

I practiced the pause and did not take any action for about two weeks. I paid attention to the breadcrumbs, which were leaning in the direction of Fortinet. I felt heartbroken that this was the case. This meant I would be leaving Cisco, a job I truly enjoyed. At first, I wanted to deny the breadcrumbs I was seeing. But, as the two weeks were coming to a close, Fortinet was the confirmation I was receiving in response to my prayer to the Universe.

The two-week pause closed when Brian called again. This time he was ready with a verbal offer, and it was strong. I knew at that moment that this was the final breadcrumb. I was sad and scared because although I've left jobs I liked, I've never left a job I loved. This was new ground.

And, it was the exact reason that I wanted to end the book with this final story. I had to put my own work to the test. I had to listen to my own advice and step into my big brave so that I could confidently facilitate change—yet again. I had to *harness my inner CEO* and stand proudly at the helm of Becca Enterprises, ready to make decisions to keep me thriving rather than surviving—even if things were good. How the outcome of this new chapter unfolds is still to be determined. However, I am looking forward with confidence, courage, and curiosity as I rise into my best season yet.

> *Final Life Hack: Opportunity will always be knocking on your door if you're just willing to answer.*

APPENDIX

| PART 1: POWER

PART 2: PASSION

PART 3: PROSPERITY

RECOMMENDED READING

It's Not About the Coffee Howard Behar

The Universe Has Your Back by Gabby Bernstein

May Cause Miracles by Gabby Bernstein

Recovery by Russell Brand

The Power of Vulnerability by Brené Brown

Wishes Fulfilled by Dr. Wayne Dyer

Eat, Pray, Love by Elizabeth Gilbert

Big Magic by Elizabeth Gilbert

Claim Your Power by Mastin Kipp

Worthy by Nancy Levin

Setting Boundaries Will Set You Free by Nancy Levin

The Ultimate Risk by Tara L. Robinson

Lean In By Sheryl Sandberg

The Body Keeps the Score by Bessel van der Kolk

A Return to Love by Marianne Williamson

Wolfpack by Abby Wambach

ACKNOWLEDGEMENTS

Writing my first book has made me realize that bringing a book to life really is a team effort. I'd like to thank my daughter, Tyler, and my son, Braydon, for always believing in me and inspiring me to be the best mom I can be. Without your love and nudging for me to do my own healing and rising from the ashes, I don't believe this book would have ever been written. I'd like to thank my husband, Jermey, for giving me the space and support to write and edit every morning for several months. Without full support and feeling that it was genuine, I'm not sure that I could have written as easily and freely as I did. Another round of family thank yous to my stepchildren, Clayton and Hailey, for your love and support. I want to thank my mother-in-law, Karla, and my sister-in-law, Jen, for being early readers and helping me elevate the story. On that note of early readers, I have to thank Connie, Monica, and Sherri for diving in as the first readers—your feedback, support, and excitement gave me the courage to bring this to life!

Next up I want to thank all of the friends, mentors, coworkers, coaches, clients, and adversaries for being a critical part of my story. Every person and every interaction weaves a thread in my tapestry of life. A special thank you to my group of closest girlfriends for supporting me during the writing process: Monica, Sherri, Connie, Jessie, Pamela, Erin, Rachel, Zue, and Julie. I love you ladies and I am beyond grateful for your encouragement. My writing soul family: Katy, Becky, Anne, Reija, and Ernesto. All six of us birthed books together in a book writers' group—an experience I didn't know I needed. My mentors for rising into a supportive role yet again: AmondaRose, Jillian, and Jen. The West and Powers side of my family—I love you all. There are more friends and family I did not get to thank individually but know how much I appreciate you!

I want to thank my developmental editor, Sarah Bossenberg with KN Literary. She was my backbone and my sanity as we structured my writing in a way that would guide others to their own transformation. My coach, Nancy Levin, for her guidance through the writing and publishing process—and for providing me a path to do another layer of healing and integration as I wrote this book. I'd like to thank another coach of mine, Mastin Kipp, for having the virtual writers' boot camp in the first place, and your other programs that have really helped me own my inner power. My publisher, Book Launchers, and everyone on that team, thank you for bringing my book to life!

To everyone on my book launch team, thank you! Special shout out to Lynae Looney at Diva PM for believing in my work and helping get it out in the world. And to all you readers, thank you for taking the time to read Harness Your Inner CEO. I am beyond grateful that you invested your time and energy not only into reading my book but for making yourself a priority!

CPSIA information can be obtained
at www.ICGtesting.com
Printed in the USA
BVHW041400051021
618194BV00014B/291

9 781737 250319